THAT NOTHING MAY BE LOST

Rev. Paul D. Scalia

That Nothing May Be Lost

Reflections on Catholic Doctrine and Devotion

IGNATIUS PRESS   SAN FRANCISCO

Cover art:
Multiplication of the Loaves and Fishes. 1505
Palacio Real, Madrid, Spain
Photo credit: Album / Art Resource, N.Y.

Cover design by Riz Boncan Marsella

© 2017 by Ignatius Press, San Francisco
All rights reserved
ISBN 978-1-62164-150-6
Library of Congress Control Number 2016956072
Printed in the United States of America ∞

CONTENTS

Appendices

FOREWORD

One of my favorite sayings over the many years of my ministry is this: there is no presence of Jesus in the world without the Church, no Church without the Eucharist, no Eucharist without the priest—and no priest without good Christian men and women who raise their sons to listen for God's calling. The story of salvation is the story of a family of vocations—lay, priestly, and religious—each needing and supporting the other on the pilgrim way to heaven. The wonderful book of essays and thoughts you now have in your hands is part diary and part guide on that road we all share.

Christian life requires a willingness to love. And I don't mean "love", the theory, or "love", the warm feeling. I mean "love", the act of will, the act of courage. Real love is always expensive. Real love is always anchored in the truth about ourselves and about others. And while the truth will make us free, nobody said it would make us comfortable. The truth is that the world is a sinful place, and we're part of that sinfulness.

This is why God sets His Chosen People apart in Baptism. This is why He sets His priests apart in the Sacrament of Holy Orders. In a way, all Christians are caught in a seeming dilemma, between the stars God calls us to reach for, and the clay we're made of. God asks us to acknowledge all of our many sins, but then He insists that we trust in His love anyway, believe in our dignity anyway, follow Him anyway, and sanctify the world anyway. And that means that if we try to do what seems so improbable—to love as Jesus loved—we're going to struggle and sometimes fail, and in failing, we'll experience the disdain of the world.

So it has always been. When the prophet Isaiah tells us that the Spirit of God has anointed him to "bind up the brokenhearted, to proclaim liberty to the captives, and the opening of the prison to those who are bound" (Is 61:1), he doesn't talk about the cost, because he's consumed with the reward of serving God—and rightly so. But Isaiah was also a sinner like the rest of us, and from the Scriptures we know that people rejected him the same way they rejected every other prophet.

The cost of discipleship can be high. Real love is always beautiful but also humbling. It asks us to listen to the needs of others and to choose what's best for them first. It asks us to admit our sins and repent of them, but it also offers the solace that we not be deterred by them. This is why discipleship is not for the fainthearted, and Christian life is an adventure meant for the brave. God needs people of selflessness and character. God needs men and women who will help Him remake the world, who will allow Him to make them into a holy people, something more than what they are without Him.

The Bible has dozens of dramatic moments, but the one that arguably matters most is from Luke 4:16–21, where Jesus identifies Himself and His mission with that same powerful passage of Isaiah 61:1: "The Spirit of the Lord is upon me, because he has anointed me to preach good news to the poor ... [and] to set at liberty those who are oppressed.... Today this Scripture has been fulfilled in your hearing" (Lk 4:18, 21). If human history has a center, this is it. If Scripture has a direction and meaning, this is it. All of God's contact with humanity either leads up to this point or flows from it. As C. S. Lewis once famously observed, in speaking these words Jesus is either stating a fact or He's blaspheming—or He's mentally ill.[1] There is no middle ground. And the people in the synagogue, who heard Him say the words, understood this very well—which is why they turned against Him.

Of course, Jesus was merely stating the truth, and His radical claim begs for a radical response. The Apostles and many others who followed Him reconfigured their lives and risked or gave away all that they owned. Joy and fruitfulness come from this kind of discipleship, but it asks from us a life of conscious focus and openness to God's Word.

The people who carried the Catholic faith forward in history, who made the culture of beauty, music, art, and architecture rooted in the Christian understanding of God and humanity—these generations were taught, spiritually fed, and shaped by priests exactly like the men who minister to us in our local Church, men not so different

---

[1] See C. S. Lewis, *Mere Christianity*, bk. 2, chap. 3, "The Shocking Alternative".

from the one who wrote this book. Where there is Catholic faith anywhere in the world, it exists because priests offered their lives for the sake of Jesus Christ and the people God called them to serve.

Today, Jesus asks each of us, not just those of us who are priests, to be His Father's word *becoming* flesh through the witness of our lives. It's through our witness—despite all our failures but guided, lifted up, and encouraged by our pastors who share our same struggles—that Christ sanctifies the world. When people see and hear us, they should see and hear Jesus Christ; and through Jesus, they will encounter the Father who loves them *despite* their sins, and our sins.

Father Scalia has written a book that deepens our faith and leads us closer to God in a hundred different ways. His good work and the powerful witness in his words remind us that we need each other's love and support as brothers and sisters in the Lord's work. Above all, it's proof that the bond of Christian people and their priests is the strength of the Church in a skeptical world that has never needed the Word of God more urgently.

+*Charles J. Chaput, O.F.M.Cap.*
Archbishop of Philadelphia

INTRODUCTION

"Gather up the Fragments Left Over, That Nothing May Be Lost"

Only one miracle is recorded by all four Gospels: the multiplication of loaves and fish (Mt 14:13–21; Mk 6:30–44; Lk 9:11–17; Jn 6:5–13). That unique unanimity alone signals the importance of the event. The miracle is indeed full of significance. By way of it our Lord shows Himself to be the new Moses, Who feeds the People of God with Bread from heaven; He reveals that He is the Messiah, Whom the crowds want to make king (see Jn 6:15); and He points us to the Eucharist, the true Bread from heaven. But for the purposes of this introduction, allow me to linger over two details of lesser importance.

First, Saint Mark tells us that when Jesus came to that deserted place and saw the crowds "he had compassion on them, because they were like sheep without a shepherd; and he began to teach them many things" (Mk 6:34; cf. Mt 9:36). We might find our Lord's response a little strange. Teaching "many things" does not strike us as a good way to respond to a vast, needy crowd. It seems odder still because we know the miracle that follows. Why pause and teach them anything? Why not cut to the chase and give them the food they need? Action is always better than dialogue, right?

Jesus knows what He is about. He is moved with pity for the crowds because they are, as we hear through the prophet Hosea, "destroyed for lack of knowledge" (Hos 4:6). It is not their physical but their spiritual hunger that moves His heart. Nor does He mourn the absence of "knowledge" as we typically think of it: the scientific, technical knowledge valued by the world, the shrewd knowledge about markets and how to get ahead. He mourns, rather, the lack of that deeper, more important knowledge—about where we come from, why we are here, and where we are going; about Who God is, what He has done for us, and that He loves us; about how we can be forgiven, healed, and saved.

The crowds suffer spiritual hunger more than physical. So He teaches first and then feeds. Indeed, His teaching is already a form of feeding. Later, when He provides food miraculously and abundantly, it is not merely to fill their bellies but to confirm His teaching as true nourishment.

Twenty centuries later, we are no different from the crowd on the shores of the Sea of Galilee. Our amazing progress in technology and science has not made us one whit smarter about the permanent things (and, many would argue, perhaps a whole lot dumber). Jesus looks upon us now, as He did the crowd then, and His heart is moved with pity. He still desires to teach us "many things", to give us the truth that nourishes.

A driving force in my vocation to the priesthood was the awareness that people were "destroyed for lack of knowledge". Not that I thought of it in those terms or had even heard of Hosea. In high school and college it usually took the form of stubbornly insisting that Church teaching was true—but without any explanation (or, I regret, much charity). Beginning in college, however, as I grew familiar with the struggles and problems afflicting people—with their wounds, addictions, loneliness, guilt, despair, etc.—I became more aware and fully convinced that the Catholic Church's teaching answered these fully, and not in some academic or "dogmatic" sense as our culture understands that word. Rather, the Church's teaching, it became clear to me, is really "saving doctrine" that brings health and peace to the soul. Without it, we are sheep without a shepherd. We spend a great deal on what fails to satisfy, while the Church extends Christ's life-giving truths freely.

The ancient Romans called a priest "pontifex"—bridge builder. And with good reason, for a priest mediates—builds a bridge—between God and man. He reconciles and establishes communion between them as a bridge between two shores. This image of the bridge builder also explains the priest as teacher. The human heart is created for the truth, and the truth is meant for the human heart. Too often we separate these two or even set them at odds with each other—thus the great "liberal" and "conservative" debates: truth versus love, dogma versus charity. In fact, these two are to be united, and it is part of a priest's duty to establish that union.

So the Church entrusts to her priests both the Catholic faith and the souls of her children. A priest's duty is to care for both. He in effect is to build a bridge, to unite and bring into communion, the truths of the faith and the souls entrusted to his care. He has the responsibility of bringing—patiently, charitably—every heart to the truth, and the truth to every heart.

Although I could not articulate this twenty-five years ago, I desired to bring souls healing, peace, and salvation by teaching the Catholic faith. After twenty years of priesthood, that conviction about the Church's teaching and the desire to communicate it have not diminished. Indeed, after years of service as a parish priest, they have only grown stronger—because a priest is privileged to see both the great depths of human suffering and the great miracles of divine grace.

Back to our Lord's miracle. After the people have eaten their fill of bread and fish, Jesus commands the Apostles, "Gather up the fragments left over, that nothing may be lost" (Jn 6:12). It is a curious command. After all, the Incarnate Word, "the King of kings and Lord of lords" (1 Tim 6:15; Rev 17:14; 19:16), need not be concerned about leftovers. If He can multiply loaves and fish as He did, why sweat the small stuff?

Well, because God created the small as well as the big. He is attentive to the little every bit as much as to the large. We get distracted by big things, and so think He does too. But His greatness is shown in the little things as well. He is happy to concern Himself with sparrows and lilies. No work of His should be taken for granted or neglected. Even the leftover crumbs and fragments are of value, because they all come from Him. "Gather up the fragments left over, that nothing may be lost."

In that light, we can say that these essays are "fragments left over". *Fragments*, because none of them is particularly long. This is no theological tome or dissertation. It will take you more time to read this introduction than any of the essays. *Left over,* because they contain nothing new. This book breaks no new ground. It contains nothing not already in the Tradition of the Church—no fresh ideas or insights. The Apostles filled twelve baskets with the fragments left over from a glorious miracle. I have tried to provide some fragments of our faith's glory.

If these writings can be fairly described as "fragments left over", their purpose corresponds to the other part of our Lord's command:

"that nothing may be lost." The Church's mission is to hand down the faith whole and entire for the salvation of souls. To neglect one dimension or the other, to cut corners here and there, only puts souls at risk. "Heresy" comes from the Greek *haireisthai*, "to choose". The heretic chooses one teaching to the exclusion of others. He fails to gather the fragments and allows truths to be lost.

Such neglect and waste is not only an intellectual failure; it endangers souls. We strive to lose nothing of Christ's truth so that souls receive the full blessing of His doctrine. Thus Blessed Paul VI: "It is an outstanding manifestation of charity toward souls to omit nothing from the saving doctrine of Christ".[1] That nothing may be lost—so that no soul may be lost.

Shortly after I was ordained, an older priest passed on sage advice: *write*. The reason for that advice was as much for the writer as for the readers. Flannery O'Connor is credited with the quip: "I write to discover what I know." Indeed, writing helps crystallize our thoughts. It forces us to articulate—and therefore to grasp better—what we already think. I have certainly found that to be true, and will be ever thankful for the advice.

But as much as I welcomed the intellectual clarity, it was not primarily for myself that I wrote. What you find in these pages is the fruit of pastoral work. They are not private musings or speculations. They have a specific audience and purpose. As for the audience, they were originally written for Catholics. But I hope that non-Catholics will find benefit in them as well. As for the purpose, they were written to communicate the truth that brings nourishment to the soul— the "saving doctrine". And it is the desire of that Heart moved with pity that all receive it.

Each essay comes from a monthly Gospel commentary, a parish bulletin, or a blog post. I am grateful to those who gave me the opportunity to write. I thank my bishop, Paul S. Loverde, without whose permission and encouragement these essays would never have been published at all—either at first or now. My gratitude to him is all the greater having worked with him directly for the past five years. Likewise, I thank Bishop Burbidge who, since his installation

[1] Pope Paul VI, Encyclical Letter *Humanae Vitae*, July 25, 1968, no. 29, http://w2.vatican.va/content/paul-vi/en/encyclicals/documents/hf_p-vi_enc_25071968_humanae-vitae.html.

as bishop of Arlington, has been so supportive of this project. Others I would like to thank are Michael Flach, editor of the *Arlington Catholic Herald*, who asked me to write a monthly Gospel commentary years ago and (even more generously) kept me on for fourteen years; Father Denis Donahue, my pastor when I was assigned at Saint Rita Parish in Alexandria, Virginia, and who permitted and encouraged me to write a weekly column for the parish bulletin; the good staff of the Diocese of Arlington blog *Encourage and Teach with Patience* that endured my delayed submissions; and Robert Royal at *The Catholic Thing*, who has welcomed my sporadic submissions for posting.

I want to express thanks to the friends who have written introductions to the different sections of this book. Each one has been, in various ways, a support and encouragement to me in my priesthood. In different ways—in conversations with them, in reading what they have written, in seeing their living of the faith—each of them has inspired me, and I am grateful for their witness in these pages.

One friend merits special mention. I first met Lizz when she was engaged to Ryan Lovett, a good Catholic man in the parish. For about a year I met with Lizz and Ryan—first to instruct her in the Catholic faith and then to prepare them for marriage. Lizz was a joy to teach. Never in my priesthood have I encountered anyone who so quickly intuited the truth of Catholic doctrine and so naturally formed her life around it. She was a living witness that the human heart is made for the truth and rejoices to find it. I had the privilege of doing their wedding and later getting to know their four children. Tragically, Lizz died last July after battling kidney cancer for several years. She was in dying as I had always known her in life—peaceful, joyful, and full of faith.

Finally, and most importantly, I thank my father and mother, who gave me the inestimable gift of the Catholic faith. When my father died suddenly last February, I came to a new realization of that gift. I will be forever (and eternally, I hope) grateful for the faith that they handed on to me. I have on my desk my father's well-worn 1960 hand missal, with funeral cards from throughout the years providing a little family history. He loved the clarity and the intellectual depth of the Church's teachings, the beauty of her liturgy, and the power of her sacraments. During the confused and confusing years after the Second Vatican Council, he and my mother made a point of finding a parish (often at some distance) that provided authentic teaching and reverent liturgy. That sacrifice spoke volumes. His fidelity to the Church's doctrine and public witness to the faith continue to inspire me—as does the memory of him standing in line for confession or kneeling in prayer after Communion, trying, like the rest of us, to recollect and avail himself of the grace of the Eucharist.

I

THE LORD

Knowing and Loving Jesus of Nazareth

Introduction

by H. James Towey

Any book on the Christian life is only of value if it facilitates or nurtures an encounter with Jesus—not the concept of Jesus or the legend of Jesus, but the Person of Jesus.

Pope Benedict XVI said, "Faith is above all a personal, intimate encounter with Jesus, and to experience his closeness, his friendship, his love; only in this way does one learn to know him ever more, and to love and follow him ever more."[1]

This encounter that Pope Benedict spoke of was foreign to me throughout my youth, even though I was a cradle Catholic and attended Catholic grade school and high school. I can attest first-hand to the danger of being "sacramentalized and catechized" but not evangelized.

As much as I had been talked to about the Catholic faith in the first twenty-eight years of my life, I had very carefully avoided a true, living relationship with God. In other words, I had not truly converted.

---

[1] Pope Benedict XVI, General Audience, October 21, 2009, quoted in "Pope Encourages Personal Relationship with Christ: Points to Example of St. Bernard of Clairvaux", Zenit.org, https://zenit.org/articles/pope-encourages-personal-relationship-with-christ/.

It took a brief meeting with Mother Teresa in Calcutta in 1985 to change the trajectory of my life and place me on the path to the Lord. It was she who introduced me to her precious Jesus in a way most unexpected.

I went to Calcutta to meet her because I was badly disillusioned with my own faith. At that point in my life, I was a standard spectator Catholic—I went to Mass and recited my rote prayers, but there was no intimacy, no real relationship with God. In truth I didn't want it. If Saint Augustine prayed along the lines of "Save me, Lord, but not just yet," my mantra was more "Let's talk someday, whatever."

I wasn't interested in a conversion, because I didn't know I needed one. I was happy worshipping myself, following my own plans and desires, tithing my time and attention to God and leaving the lion's share to myself. I just wasn't that interested in what God had to say in Scripture or Church teaching. I was very comfortable in my hypocrisy. I said I was a Catholic, but I really wasn't much of one.

Now, the great thing about being a hypocrite is that you can spot hypocrisy in people in a millisecond. So I was sitting in judgment of everybody, criticizing bishops and churchgoers and all those whom I felt weren't measuring up.

But out in the distance was this one person, this tiny nun, Mother Teresa of Calcutta, who didn't appear to me to be a hypocrite but actually seemed to be living the Gospel. She spoke about Jesus as if He were next to her or actually in her heart. So I wanted to meet her; because I was going to be in Asia on a business trip, I thought it would be cool to swing by India and meet her on the way home.

The problem was, Calcutta was full of poor people, and I didn't want to be around poor people. They made me uncomfortable. They made demands on me. They made me feel guilty. I couldn't fix their lives, and I didn't want to be around what I deemed were suffering, hopeless people.

So how could I get to Mother Teresa and meet her without being around poor people? Well, it was impossible. So the deal I made with myself was as follows: I'd go into Calcutta to meet Mother Teresa, and then on the way back to America, stop in Hawaii for five days. That's how I assembled enough courage to go to God-forsaken Calcutta—for barely a full day. And that's what I did.

On August 20, 1985, in the headquarters of Mother Teresa's nuns and just outside the chapel where they had Mass, I met tiny Mother

Teresa. Despite turning seventy-five years old that week, she bounded into the hallway to meet me like a young schoolgirl. She was everything I wasn't. She was focused and serious and cheerful and fully alive. There was an aura to her that was unmistakable. She asked me if I had been to her home for the dying. I told her no, I had not. I didn't tell her that I had absolutely no intention of doing so, but when she told me to go there and see the Sister in charge, how could I say, "No, thanks"?

I arrived at this home for the dying, probably the most important Christian mission of the twentieth century, and met the nun in charge. To my utter disbelief, she thought I had come to volunteer! So she handed me some medicine and cotton and said, "Go and clean the man in bed forty-six that has scabies."

I was busted, trapped. I couldn't say, "Well, I'd love to, but I have to be leaving," because I had just arrived. So it was pride, pure pride, that got me to assent and go to bed forty-six, because not a part of me wanted to touch the man lying there.

But when I touched him, something changed. I didn't hear an angelic chorus singing. In fact, I was happy to get out of the home as soon as I could. Yet I had read Mother Teresa's words describing "Jesus in his distressing disguise of the poor".[2] And in the years that followed, I came to realize that when I had touched the man in bed forty-six, Jesus had touched me back. He had been waiting there for me, all those wasted years. My conversion had begun.

I have asked myself many times why I was privileged to meet Mother Teresa, get to know her personally, and work with her and her wonderful Sisters and priests for twelve years. Indeed I met my wife at Mother Teresa's AIDS home in Washington, where we both volunteered. I wouldn't have my wife or my five children in my life if it were not for that fateful day thirty years ago. Why me? I know I didn't deserve any of this. I remember exactly who I was the day I met Mother Teresa, and how I was too proud to admit that I didn't want to touch that poor man—so I have no illusions about who I was then or am now.

But if the Lord allowed me this relationship with Mother, it was clearly meant for others. All told, it was God's mercy—the God Who

[2] Mother Teresa, *In the Heart of the World: Thoughts, Stories, and Prayers* (Novato, Calif.: New World Library, 1997); see also https://thomasaquinas.edu/about/bl-mother-teresa%E2%80%99s-commencement-address-class-1982.

seeks out the lost, Who seeks out the hypocrite, Who is the friend of sinners like me—that brought me to Mother Teresa.

You don't have to go to Calcutta to find Jesus. As Mother Teresa said, Calcutta is everywhere if you have eyes to see.

H. James Towey

Hearth, Home, and Holiness

The ancient Romans prized the virtue of piety—that simple devotion to one's family, country, gods, and to all that bestows and shapes one's life. The poet Virgil knew this and repeatedly described Aeneas, Rome's legendary founder, as *pious*. This sturdy virtue served Rome well and provided the basis for a nation that would shape the world for centuries.

At the Incarnation, God takes on the virtue of piety. For the pagans the pious man was devoted to the gods. For Christians, God Himself is pious—devoted to His Mother and father; to His family, town, and country; to the religion, customs, and traditions of His people. Jesus is both the Lord of Israel and her devoted Son. In the ancient chant *Te Deum*, the Church praises Jesus, saying, "You did not spurn the Virgin's womb." Nor did He spurn Mary's modest home, Joseph's workshop, Nazareth, Galilee, or even the troublesome, backward Galileans.

We see our Lord's piety especially in the thirty years of His "hidden life" with Joseph and Mary. But He did not set aside this virtue when He began His public life. After His manifestation at His Baptism in the Jordan[3] and His victory over the devil's temptations in the desert (Mt 4:1–11; Mk 1:12–13; Lk 4:1–13), we would think He was ready for the big time, for Jerusalem, and then perhaps Athens and Rome, and then—but no. "Jesus returned ... into Galilee.... And he came to Nazareth, where he had been brought up" (Lk 4:14, 16; cf. Mt 4:12; Mk 1:14). He willed to begin the work of salvation in His hometown, in the old neighborhood, in the synagogue, that old familiar building He visited every Sabbath, "as was his custom" (Lk 4:16).

Christ teaches us what it means to be human, and then divine. And so it is with the virtue of piety. He has taken this earthy, sturdy, unsophisticated quality and made it His own. In so doing He teaches us its importance and gives it eternal value. In our work of sanctification we should not consider piety beyond us. As we strive for the higher virtues, we do not spurn this humble one. Devotion to God as Father

---

[3] "This is my beloved Son" (Mt 3:17; Mk 9:7; cf. Lk 3:22).

and the Church as Mother comes more easily for those who first have piety toward one's mom and dad. "Charity begins at home", the saying goes. Indeed it does, because Incarnate Love Himself began at home. So must we.

Unfortunately, the American mind-set of "striking out on your own" can work against piety. Instead of being devoted to kith and kin, we grow tired of them and of all things familiar. We see them as things to depart from and leave behind as we "make it big". Our technology and media detach us even more from hearth and home. We give less attention to where we are and with whom than we do to some event or person miles away. A culture that uses the absurd phrase "virtual community" will not have the virtue of piety but only virtual piety.

Good old George Bailey proclaimed, "I'm shakin' the dust of this crummy little town off my feet and I'm gonna see the world!"[4] He learned his lesson eventually. Our Lord, however, never had such a desire. He loved His family and town. He chose fellow Galileans as His Apostles. He did not shake the dust of His little town off His feet but brought it with Him. He went up to Jerusalem not to "make it big" but to complete the humble work—and the work of humility—begun in Nazareth. May we likewise devote ourselves to the simplicity of those household goods—of hearth and home—that we may in turn find a dwelling in God's house.

The Victory of the Baptized

If we think at all about our Lord's temptation in the desert, we probably think that it came about by chance. We imagine Jesus in the desert, fasting and praying, minding His own business, when along comes the devil to tempt Him. In fact, both Matthew and Luke tell us clearly that Jesus went into the desert to be "tempted by the devil" (Mt 4:1; Lk 4:2). It was not happenstance or coincidence. His purpose for going into the desert was to be tempted. This might strike

---

[4] *It's a Wonderful Life*, directed by Frank Capra (Hollywood: Liberty Films, 1946).

us as odd because, well, we ought to avoid temptations. But the Redeemer seeks them out—to triumph over them on our behalf and so give us an example. He goes to be tempted, therefore, not for His own sake but for ours.

Notice that His temptation immediately follows His Baptism. These two events—separated in our minds by different Sundays or new chapter headings—are closely joined in the Gospels. In a sense, it is because of His Baptism that He goes into the desert to be tempted. At His Baptism Jesus identifies Himself with sinful humanity. In the desert He experiences the temptations of sinful humanity. He is tempted, as He was baptized, for our sake.

He allows Himself to be tempted to give us an example. By His resistance He teaches us how to resist temptations. Again, this has everything to do with His Baptism. Notice His childlike simplicity and obedience. He possesses complete confidence and trust in His Father. He has come directly from His Baptism, where He heard the Father say of Him, "This is my beloved Son, with whom I am well pleased" (Mt 3:17; cf. Lk 3:22). Those words give us a sense of the trust granted to our Lord's human soul. In His confrontation with Satan, then, Jesus does not rely on His own strength or wisdom; He rests secure in the Father's words at the Jordan.

And not only at the Jordan. In response to each assault of the devil, Jesus quotes the words of Scripture with a childlike confidence in their power to save. He does not enter into a debate or a dialogue with the devil. He does not prove Himself smarter or more clever. He does not outwit or overwhelm the devil. His responses are amazingly childlike, as we might expect from a Man Whose eternal Sonship was just revealed. Indeed, we might miss the power of His responses precisely because they lack any worldly sophistication or shrewdness. Their power lies in their simplicity. They speak of that childlike trust in and devotion to His Father; quoting Deuteronomy, Jesus tells the devil, "Man shall not live by bread alone, but by every word that proceeds from the mouth of God.... You shall not tempt the Lord your God.... You shall worship the Lord your God and him only shall you serve" (Mt 4:4, 7, 10; quoting Deut 8:3; 6:16, 13).

How different we are. We think we can outwit or withstand the devil. We carelessly place ourselves in occasions of sin. Instead of dismissing sinful situations and suggestions immediately, we enter into that dangerous dialogue with the devil. We allow doubt to enter our minds about the Word of God, parsing Scripture in a worldly manner and providing the evil one with more and more room to maneuver. We consider ourselves either smart enough to figure out his temptations or strong enough to resist them. Sooner or later we learn that we are not quite as smart as Old Scratch, nor as persevering.

Our Lord's simplicity teaches us to trust less in our own virtues and more in our status as children of God. Consider again the connection between His Baptism and His temptation. The Father's love revealed at His Baptism provided His human soul with the confidence to rest securely in His Father's care, and by that means to thwart the devil's attacks. We have access to that same grace by way of our own Baptism. Everything necessary to triumph over temptation was granted us at Baptism. We need only stir up that same straightforward, disarming confidence in the Father's love, allowing ourselves to be simple and childlike—and therefore victorious.

The Same Old Thing

Have you ever noticed how ordinary our Lord was? The Word Incarnate, the Second Person of the Trinity, possessing the fullness of humanity, appeared to be an ordinary man. There was no halo around His head, no divine light emanating from Him, no choir of angels attending Him. His voice did not resound with a heavenly boom or echo. We have no reason to believe that His carpentry set new standards for woodwork. He seemed to be the same as everyone else.

It was precisely this ordinariness that shocked the people of Nazareth. Having heard about His miracles in other places, they were no longer content with the ordinary Jesus Who grew up there. "Is not this Joseph's son?" (Lk 4:22), they asked, perhaps with disappointment. They wanted someone different, some display of power and grandeur—something out of the ordinary. Our Lord knew their thoughts: "[W]hat we have heard you did at Capernaum, do here also in your own country" (Lk 4:23).

We should not fault the people of Nazareth too severely. They simply fell into a common trap in religion: what C. S. Lewis calls "the horror of the Same Old Thing".[5] Theirs is a cautionary tale. We can easily grow impatient with the slow, steady, everyday process of growth and sanctification. We want something new and improved, like everything else we have. Saint Paul saw this danger, warning of the day "when people will not endure sound teaching, but having itching ears they will accumulate for themselves teachers to suit their own likings, and will turn away from listening to the truth and wander into myths" (2 Tim 4:3–4).

It happens just as Saint Paul predicted. To satisfy the itch for novelty, people seek the most recent apparition, the latest theology, or the trendiest method of prayer. Tired of the apostolic faith, they find (or invent) a "new" Catholicism for the chimerical "modern man". For example, look at how people treat the Mass. One group or another always seems to attach gimmicks or an agenda to the Mass, instead of allowing it to stand on its own. Like the people of Nazareth, they want something new and different.

To overcome this affliction, we do well to recall the ordinariness of our Lord. Yes, He worked many miracles. But He spent the majority of His life (thirty of His thirty-three years) in the humdrum, common, everyday world. He prayed, worked, ate, slept, and played as everyone else did. Perhaps we call this His "hidden life" not so much because it is unknown as because it is unremarkable.

His life sets the pattern for our faith. Yes, God still works miracles. But He comes to us most frequently and powerfully through the common and familiar things: the Creed, the Mass, confession, the Rosary, the Ten Commandments, etc. These are the basics, the same old things. Our growing weary of them comes not from any defect on their part, but only from a lack of faith on ours.

These same old things work entirely to our benefit because they increase our faith. Miracles encourage the faithful. But the virtue of faith increases more when we encounter the same old things and believe what is unseen—that is, when we look at the pouring of water and see the infusion of divine life; when we hear the words of absolution and trust that we are forgiven; when we learn the teaching of the

[5] C. S. Lewis, *The Screwtape Letters* (San Francisco: HarperSanFrancisco, 2001), 135.

Church and receive it as the revelation of God Himself; when we gaze upon the Host and adore It as our Lord and our God.

A Cry of the Heart

In the Catholic Church the month of June is traditionally devoted to the Sacred Heart of Jesus. During this time the Church calls her children to reflect on His Heart as the symbol not only of His love for us but also of His loneliness and suffering due to our neglect. As He said to Saint Margaret Mary Alacoque, the Apostle of the Sacred Heart: "Behold the Heart which has so loved men that it has spared nothing, even to exhausting and consuming Itself, in order to testify Its love; and in return, I receive from the greater part only ingratitude"— good words to consider on the Solemnity of the Sacred Heart, which typically falls in June.

Then, later in the same month, on June 29, the Solemnity of Saints Peter and Paul, we hear a similar plaintive cry: "[W]ho do you say that I am?" (Mt 16:15; Mk 8:29; Lk 9:20). Our Lord asks this question certainly to elicit Simon Peter's profound confession of faith: "You are the Christ, the Son of the living God" (Mt 16:16). And we cannot overstate the doctrinal implications of the question and its necessary answer. But we should also hear His words another way—not as God quizzing men but as the God-Man appealing to men. We can hear them as a cry from a man's heart—in this case, from the Sacred Heart.

"Who do you say that I am?" We all desire to be known by those we love. Love seeks to be reciprocated and thus shared. Knowing the other and being known is essential. That is why we seek to console those we love by saying, "I know", or "I understand." Those words do not alleviate the pain or remove its cause. But they bring relief by assuring those suffering that they are not alone. Great pain can be endured if we know that we are accompanied by those who know and understand us. The greatest pain and loneliness come when one is not known, not understood.

Everyone desires to be known by those he loves. And our Lord is no exception. "Who do you say that I am?" When He asks this question He had already been preaching, teaching, and healing for some time. He had just heard—with some dismay, to be sure—the weak answer to His question "Who do men say that the Son of man is?" (Mt 16:13). The crowds who followed Him so eagerly did not know Him. They thought He was someone else: "John the Baptist, . . . Elijah, . . . Jeremiah, or one of the prophets" (Mt 16:14). So He turns to His closest friends, the Apostles, His constant companions, and hoping to find some solace in their understanding—that they, at least, got it—He asks, "Who do you say that I am?"

The question has a corollary at the end of our Lord's Bread of Life discourse (see Jn 6:25–71). Watching the murmuring crowds abandon Him, He again turns to His Apostles and asks, "Will you also go away?" (Jn 6:67). At that moment also His Heart cries out for someone who would know and accompany Him. At that moment also Peter steps forward for all the Apostles and consoles the Sacred Heart: "Lord, to whom shall we go? You have the words of eternal life; and we have believed, and have come to know, that you are the Holy One of God" (Jn 6:68–69).

"Who do you say that I am?" Our response to this question certainly determines our faith and our very salvation. But it also has great meaning for our Lord's Sacred Heart. Our faithful response consoles Him, brings some degree of relief to His loneliness and suffering. The Sacred Heart teaches us that coming to know Jesus Christ is not just a matter of catechesis or providing for our own salvation. Coming to know Him—indeed, merely desiring to know Him—comforts Him for all the neglect and indifference He suffers.

"Who do you say that I am?" We learn how to respond to this question from the two Apostles who close out the month of June. Saint Peter's doctrinal response—"You are the Christ, the Son of the living God"—shows that a simple act of faith pleases and consoles the One Who came to give Himself to us. Saint Paul's intense longing—"[T]hat I may know him," he simply prays (Phil 3:10)—teaches us that coming to know Jesus is ongoing. At no point should we stop desiring to know Him.

In a profound sense, our Lord must suffer the loneliness of not being entirely known. No one can know Him perfectly. And yet—amazingly—our simple faith and our mere desire to know Him consoles His Sacred Heart. Peter's inspired response and Paul's longing brought Him genuine joy and consolation. May we imitate the Apostles in our profession of faith and our striving to know Him more.

Drawn

Little Lucette was inexplicably drawn to the man on the cross—inexplicably, because she had no idea who he was or why he was crucified. Her parents had banished from her life any knowledge of or reference to God. But a gift catalog had slipped through their defenses, and Lucette found in those pages a little crucifix. By an interior grace she knew that he had died for others—for her. She secretly tore out the page and would often gaze devoutly—and covertly—at the man on the cross. Over the years her devotion matured into love. She learned Who the Man on the Cross was, and she gave herself to Him in religious life, dying not too long ago as Mother Veronica Namoyo of the Poor Clares.

As amazing as the story is (told by Mother herself in *A Memory for Wonders*[6]), it seems to be just what our Lord promised: "[A]nd I, when I am lifted up from the earth, will draw all men to myself" (Jn 12:32). That curious phrase—"lifted up"—occurs twice in John's Gospel (cf. Jn 3:14; 12:32). It is the phrase Jesus uses to describe His Crucifixion: "He said this to show by what death he was to die" (Jn 12:33). Being nailed to the Cross and then raised is indeed being "lifted up". The original Greek word has the sense of being raised up in order to be seen—of being exalted (*exaltatus* in the Latin). We first hear that He is exalted—so "that whoever believes in him may have eternal life" (Jn 3:15).

His Crucifixion is indeed a form of exaltation. Like the raising of a trophy or medal, the "lifting up" of our Lord announces victory. It proclaims God's mercy and the sacrifice that reconciles us with Him. Christ upon the Cross reveals the God powerful enough to allow Himself to be pierced, powerful enough to be merciful. We

---

[6] Mother Veronica Namoyo Le Goulard, *A Memory for Wonders: A True Story* (San Francisco: Ignatius Press, 1993).

encounter Jesus' greatness not so much in His miracles and teachings as in the sacrifice to which they point and from which they derive all meaning and power. Thus the Apostle resolves "to know nothing ... except Jesus Christ and him crucified" (1 Cor 2:2).

By this exaltation, He promises, "I ... will draw all men to myself." And so indeed we are drawn to Christ crucified. We place the crucifix on our walls and wear it about our necks. Despite the horror of public execution, and of that particular form, we find the crucifix attractive. Something about Christ on the Cross draws us, makes us view it as good and beautiful. What draws us, of course, is the self-giving and self-sacrifice we find there. In looking upon Christ crucified, we see His words embodied and confirmed: "For God so loved the world that he gave his only-begotten Son" (Jn 3:16). "Greater love has no man than this, that a man lay down his life for his friends" (Jn 15:13).

Being drawn *to* Christ on the Cross implies also being drawn *away* from something. The Greek word for "draw" implies a certain forcefulness, that this drawing is also a snatching away from someone. Indeed, our Lord on the Cross—in the power of His humiliation—snatches us away from the evil one. The exaltation of Christ crucified is of course a weapon against vice and the devil. The more we gaze upon the One Who died for us, the more we leave sin behind and cling to Him.

He draws *everyone* to Himself on the Cross. Christ crucified is the unifying principle of our faith, what makes the Church one. Impolite though it may be to observe, we do not gather at Mass because we are friends or even acquaintances. No, Christian unity goes deeper than worldly connections. We come together because we come to Him as sinners in need of salvation. Every single one of us must come to the Cross of Christ. First we come in sorrow, placing ourselves before the judgment seat of Christ, where all our sins are laid bare. But then we come to Him in joy, giving thanks for the sacrifice that has set us free from sin and snatched us from the evil one.

"Behold the wood of the Cross, on which hung the salvation of the world." Catholics hear those words every year, as the Cross is lifted up—exalted—in the Good Friday liturgy of the Lord's Passion. Then we are drawn to Christ on the Cross and respond, "Come let us adore." Let us pray now to be freed from what still ensnares us so that we can be more fully drawn to Him.

Time and Timelessness

A good teacher lets his students know the time of their tests. He may on occasion surprise them with a pop quiz, but he will make certain they know the date and time of the final exam. Our Lord, however, does just the opposite. Regarding His Second Coming and the Last Judgment (a final exam if ever there was one), He says "of that day or that hour, no one knows" (Mk 13:32). Now, this seems like the kind of thing He should want us to know, so that we can prepare. So why does He not reveal the day or the hour?

He remains silent on this issue because our fallen human nature needs this strong medicine. Original Sin has produced in us the tendency to procrastinate—that is, to prefer the immediate pleasure of some diversion to the labor that produces a future good. We would rather play video games than do homework, check our Facebook page than pray, watch football than rake the leaves.

And we should not think that we would treat our Lord's return any differently. If we knew the precise day and hour of His coming, would we spend the time between now and then preparing for it? Would we strive to increase in grace and good works in anticipation of His arrival? No, probably not. If we knew the time of His coming, we would most likely leave our repentance and prayer for the day before—at the earliest.

Saint Augustine, who knew a thing or two about delay, warns us: "God has promised forgiveness to your repentance, but He has not promised tomorrow to your procrastination."[7] Jesus keeps the day and hour hidden from us so that we will always be on the watch and (one hopes) always prepared—indeed, always preparing. He has not promised us tomorrow precisely so that we will prepare now, not at the eleventh hour. It is strong medicine against our procrastination. He keeps us ignorant of His coming so that we will be always preparing for it.

Our ignorance of His return also brings us a great good. It frees us from slavery to the world's schedule. Few things control our lives

---

[7] Augustine of Hippo, reported in Josiah Hotchkiss Gilbert, *Dictionary of Burning Words of Brilliant Writers* (1895), 486.

more than the schedule, calendar, and time clock. We need to free ourselves from these. Certainly, we must keep a good calendar, be punctual, and all the rest. The problem is, we get overwhelmed by the tyranny of time, allowing the world instead of our Lord to determine our schedule. Without a fixed point of reference or purpose, we easily collapse under time's relentless march.

The possibility of Jesus coming at any moment relativizes temporal matters and reveals Him as Lord of all time. Time only has meaning in relation to Him and should be arranged with Him in view. As the Church prays at the Easter Vigil, "All time belongs to Him and all the ages." Our vigilance for His arrival puts the world's schedule in perspective. All time gives way to His return. For that reason, we should schedule into our daily routine set moments of prayer— the Morning Offering, the Angelus, the Rosary, the Liturgy of the Hours, etc. These pauses in our day allow our Lord to break into our time, and they remind us that the world's schedule does not rule us. They are ways of putting time in its proper place—in service of Him.

"Of that day or that hour, no one knows." The sober awareness of our Lord's sudden and unexpected return curbs our procrastination and frees us to live for eternity. Yes, we should continue to schedule appointments, keep the calendar, and observe our routine. All the while, however, we remain free from time's tyranny, ready to cancel all else, and prepared for that most important appointment—the moment of His return.

Unmiraculous Miracles

What does it mean when a miracle is not, well, miraculous? That is, when a miracle does not have the drama, excitement, or big production qualities that we might expect? Certainly, some miracles have plenty of drama—voices from heaven, seas parting, fires descending, and so on. But we also know of simple, subtle miracles. Elijah, after all, encountered God not in the wind, nor the earthquake, nor the fire, but in the "still small voice" (1 Kings 19:12). Indeed, the two most important miracles—the Incarnation and the Resurrection—are notable for their subtlety and hiddenness: the quiet of Bethlehem, the simple presence in the upper room.

Our Lord's raising of the son of the widow of Nain provides another example (see Lk 7:11–17). Yes, our Lord did something extraordinary in raising a man from the dead. Yes, "[f]ear seized them all" (Lk 7:16). They exclaimed, "God has visited his people!" (Lk 7:16), and the "report concerning him spread through the whole of Judea and all the surrounding country" (Lk 7:17). Nevertheless, the miracle possesses an extraordinary simplicity. Our Lord encounters the funeral procession. He is moved with pity and tells the mother, "Do not weep" (Lk 7:13). He steps forward, touches the coffin, and says, "Young man, I say to you, arise" (Lk 7:14). The man sits up, begins to speak, and then, in the most touching detail, Jesus "gave him to his mother" (Lk 7:15). No angels, no voices from heaven, no earthquakes, no lightning—only the man Jesus giving two commands.

What does it mean when a miracle is not miraculous? First, it calls our attention to our Lord's humanity. By His divine nature He performs the miracle. But He is moved to do so in His human nature. That He was moved with pity refers to His Sacred Heart and His capacity to be moved with human love. Saint Luke tells us that the deceased was "the only son of his mother, and she was a widow" (Lk 7:12). This describes our Lord Himself, and His Mother. So it should not surprise us that He turns first to the widow, in whom He sees the anticipation of Mary's sorrow. "Do not weep," He tells her—as if to tell His own Mother. Yes, our Lord is all-powerful. But in His sacred humanity He places Himself within our reach, so that our misery moves Him to act on our behalf.

Second, the unremarkable miracle reminds us of grace's power working through simple means. Our Lord raises the dead with a simple command—spoken in regular, human words. No choir of angels, no thundering voice, no divine megaphone. He continues to do so today through the ministry of the Church—through the all too simple words of her all too simple ministers. We should not doubt the power of words—of truth spoken in charity—to console, heal, transform, and above all raise.

We find this miraculous simplicity especially in the Sacrament of Penance, in which Jesus uses the humanity of the priest to raise a soul from the dead. First, by simply receiving the penitent, the confessor in effect steps forward and touches the coffin. He halts the procession of death that sin has begun. By the words of absolution the priest commands the soul to arise. And just as in Nain Jesus raised a young man, so in the confessional the priest—or, rather, Jesus through the priest—restores our youth. He rejuvenates our souls.

Nor did Jesus allow the miracle of raising a man from the dead to obscure the importance of the man's human relationships. He "gave him to his mother". So also now, the miracle of Reconciliation is also attentive to our relationships. It accomplishes not only our spiritual resurrection but also our restoration to one another, the healing of relationships. Or, viewed differently, as our Lord gave the man back to his mother, so Penance restores us to Mother Church, to her who—like the widow of Nain for her son—brought us to new birth, nourished us, and mourned our death in sin.

Yes, God at times works through the extraordinary. But His preferred way of acting is through the simple ministries of the Church— the faith taught, the sacraments celebrated. While we should not reject the possibility of the dramatic, we should tune our souls to find our Lord in His subtle approaches, in the humble gestures and simple words that console and give life.

Take a Deep Breath

When we think of the gift of the Holy Spirit, we typically think of Pentecost—the Spirit descending upon Mary and the Apostles in the upper room. We therefore often overlook an earlier scene. On Easter Sunday, when Jesus appeared to the Apostles, "[H]e breathed on them, and said to them, 'Receive the Holy Spirit'" (Jn 20:22). Of course, we should not set these two events in opposition to each other. Pentecost holds pride of place as the solemn and definitive descent of the Holy Spirit. Nevertheless, by giving the Spirit also on Easter Sunday, Jesus reveals certain truths about the Spirit.

First, intimacy. "He breathed on them"—an unusual gesture, then as now. To breathe on someone requires being close. To give the Spirit Jesus had to be close to the Apostles, right next to them. He was in their "personal space", because His gift was intensely personal. Breath, after all, comes from within. It indicates the interior life of a person. In bestowing the Spirit, Jesus gives an intimate gift. The Spirit is not a gift external to Him but proceeding from deep within Him.

Second, life. Breath indicates life. Thus we have the term "life breath". When someone has stopped breathing, we may perform mouth-to-mouth resuscitation, giving our breath so that he will have life. What we accomplish on a biological, physical level, our Lord accomplishes in the spiritual. We once were lifeless bodies, devoid of life breath. As once He breathed life into Adam (see Gen 2:7), now He breathes His life—His Spirit—into us. But His breath now brings eternal life.

Third, power. By bestowing this gift on Easter Sunday, our Lord associates the Spirit with His Resurrection. This manifests the Spirit's power. This is the "Spirit of him who raised Jesus from the dead". This Spirit also has the power to raise us up: the one "who raised Jesus from the dead will give life to your mortal bodies also" (Rom 8:11). So Saint Paul tells us, "God did not give us a spirit of timidity but a spirit of power and love and self-control" (2 Tim 1:7).

Our Lord does not ration His gift of the Spirit (see Jn 3:34). We, however, ration our reception of the Spirit. We remain apart from the Giver, and we do not trust enough in the Spirit's power. Instead of drawing close to Jesus, we keep Him at arm's length. We acknowledge Him from afar and perhaps call out our needs to Him. It is, we cynically think, nice to have Him in our lives. But we do not draw close enough to feel His breath. We like our illusion of independence and do not want Him breathing down our necks. And instead of trustfully surrendering to the Spirit's power, we seek merely His assistance. We should pray to the Holy Spirit for holiness. But we do not think that possible and settle for lesser things.

A gift ought to be received in the manner it is given. As regards the gift of the Spirit, this means drawing close to Jesus. We need to be up close and personal, next to His face, feeling His breath upon us. The Gift He gives is personal, from His very Heart, and He desires to give this Gift to each of us personally. In asking for the Spirit, we should do so with confidence in the Spirit's power. The Holy Spirit raises from the dead and—even more incredibly—changes sinners into saints. It makes no sense to ask for the Holy Spirit without intending to be made holy. Therefore, let us draw close to Jesus, to receive His breath, to receive the Spirit of holiness.

II

THE CHURCH

Knowing and Loving the Body of Christ

Introduction

by Gloria Purvis

My experience of the Church has been a continuing call to reject what is comfortable and customary for something else. The Church invites us to grow in love with the Lord—a lesson, a calling that comes to each of us in its own time.

I was born and raised in Charleston, South Carolina. Catholics were, and are still, a minority. Of that minority, some were African American. Although we were not Catholic, my parents chose to send me and my sisters to the former Cathedral School because they valued education and believed it offered the best academic opportunity in the city. It was here that I encountered the Catholic Church.

The Cathedral School was nearly 100 percent African American but no less Catholic. I cherished the prayers and devotions and particularly my teachers, the Oblate Sisters of Providence who wore their full habits. I learned my three Rs and much about the truth and beauty of the faith. It was a happy experience.

And while I treasured these experiences, I naturally followed the faith of my family who were members of the Centenary Methodist Episcopal Church. However, I had a profound personal encounter when I was twelve years old that upended my entire life.

During lunch my classmates had a food fight in the cafeteria, which we dutifully cleaned afterward. This process sobered us up for the inevitable conversation we would have to have with Sister Carmelita, who served both as religion teacher and the principal at the time. As we sat rigidly in our desks dreading our punishment, Sister Carmelita sat behind the teacher's desk and asked each of us one by one if we had participated in that food fight. She gave us the opportunity to admit or deny our guilt publicly. One by one, we admitted our guilt. Sister Carmelita was growing more and more annoyed with each, "Yes, Sister, I did it."

With the last affirmation, she declared that we had to accompany her to church and sit in absolute silence and stillness while she conversed with God. No one made a sound. We walked single file over to the lower church of the cathedral and filled up the pews quietly. I could see Sister Carmelita working something out in prayer. I could see her hand motions and her veil swishing as she moved. I thought we might have pushed her to her breaking point in practicing the virtue of patience.

I focused my eyes on the monstrance on the altar. At that moment, my body was consumed by fire. I felt its warmth but no pain or burn. I came to know that Jesus Christ was real and alive in the Blessed Sacrament. It was an immediate, unexpected, personal encounter with Jesus Christ in the Holy Eucharist. It was an unforgettable and indescribable experience.

Several days later, Sister Carmelita announced that the Catholic students would soon prepare for Confirmation. I approached Sister Carmelita and told her, "I think I am supposed to be Catholic." She did not accept my pronouncement and wisely instructed me to ask my parents. Instead, I went home to inform my parents that I was becoming a Catholic.

After a few seconds of silence, my mother informed me that I would have to attend Mass every Sunday and Holy Days of Obligation, abstain from meat on Fridays, pray my Rosary, and on and on. To her surprise, I agreed.

Thereafter, I practiced my faith on my own, but I knew I was where I belonged. I belonged to Jesus, and He had stretched out His loving hand to me through the Church. By accepting that hand, the

Church accepted me. He had reached out to me in an extraordinary way to get my attention. That meant something to me.

As I matured, I realized my faith was the only salve for my brokenness, for my struggles and challenges—and the Church was the place for this consolation and healing. Because of my faith I was able to bear many crosses from my older sister's unexpected death in her early twenties, to my own infertility, to my mother's near-death experience. The pain was palpable, and sometimes crippling, but bearable only because of my relationship with Christ and the aid the Church gave me in those difficulties.

I talked with the saints—our older brothers and sisters in the faith—for help with my particular trials. When my mind was not focused on the correct thing, the Lord would sometimes intervene gently and at other times not so gently. Once, as a married adult, when I was leaving the confessional, I glanced at a statue of Saint Anthony and I heard his voice say, "Why don't you ask me to help you regain your lost virtue?" I was stunned and deeply pondered this question in my heart. I am still asking Saint Anthony for help in that regard.

The Catholic Church is often called the Mother Church, and rightly so. She nurtures her children with the sacraments, clothes us in her forgiveness, showers us with hope and faith, and brings us closer to salvation. When we are at peace and seek love, we are in unison with her. And when we are in accordance with her, we are healing and uniting the Body of Christ.

Yet even when we fail, when we are afraid, or struggling to overcome our selfish interests, we must realize that the Lord is there to love us and help us and forgive us. But we must be willing to reject what is not pleasing to Him when we approach Him in the Sacrament of Reconciliation. This understanding helps us examine our motives. I know that I am not a particularly special soul, just broken. In that brokenness, I have encountered the merciful, loving, just God through His Church. May I, and each individual she calls, be near her always and seek Him in the sacraments, the Word, and in dying to self.

Gloria Purvis

Catholics Believe

"Being Christian is not the result of an ethical choice or a lofty idea, but the encounter with an event, a person, which gives life a new horizon and a decisive direction," wrote Pope Benedict XVI in his first encyclical, *Deus Caritas Est*.[1] And, as if a follow-up to that, he soon after published *Jesus of Nazareth*,[2] an in-depth examination of the man who defines Christian life. Following the Pope's lead, then, it would be enough to say simply, "Catholics believe in Jesus." At the center of all Catholic doctrine, liturgy, morality, and prayer is the Person of Jesus.

With all Christians, Catholics believe that Jesus is the Savior and the Son of God. As Savior, he rescues us from eternal death. We were cut off and dead through sin. He has reconciled us with the Father, establishing peace through "the blood of his cross" (Col 1:20). By His death He paid the price for us and won for us every grace necessary for forgiveness, sanctification, and salvation.

But His redemption is more than merely a restoration. It is also an elevation. As the Son of God, Jesus brings us into the intimate life of the Trinity. Through the Holy Spirit He gives us a participation in His own Sonship. We become "sons in the Son", or as the traditional phrase has it, "partakers of the divine nature" (2 Pet 1:4). To be Catholic, then, means to live a Trinitarian life—to live according to the Spirit, in the likeness of the Son, for the glory of the Father.

Salvation and sonship—these are what Jesus won for us. Yet these gifts must still be extended throughout the world and throughout history. He desires that every soul encounter Him, that He be formed in every soul (cf. Gal 4:19). To accomplish this, Jesus established His Church. (And it is on this point that Catholics differ from most other Christian denominations.) When Jesus ascended into heaven, He did not leave behind a book, or even instructions to write a book. Rather, He left behind a hierarchical community of believers, His

[1] Pope Benedict XVI, Encyclical Letter *Deus Caritas Est*, December 25, 2005, no. 1, http://w2.vatican.va/content/benedict-xvi/en/encyclicals/documents/hf_ben-xvi_enc_20051225_deus-caritas-est.html.

[2] Pope Benedict XVI, *Jesus of Nazareth: From the Baptism in the Jordan to the Transfiguration* (New York: Doubleday, 2007).

Church. And He established this not as a merely human organization but as His abiding presence in the world—as His Body animated by His Spirit. Thus we believe that one's personal relationship with Jesus is inseparable from the Church.

We believe this union of Christ and the Church on the authority of Jesus Himself. "He who hears you hears me," He said to His disciples. "[A]nd he who rejects you rejects me" (Lk 10:16). Similarly, when the risen Lord confronted Saul of Tarsus, He identified Himself with His Church: "[W]hy do you persecute *me*?" (Acts 9:4; italics added). And again, "I am Jesus, whom you are persecuting" (Acts 9:5; cf. Acts 9:1–19; 22:6–11; 26:2–18). The lesson was not wasted. Years later Saul, by then the Apostle Paul, described the union between Christ and the Church: they are two in one flesh, head and members, bridegroom and bride (see 1 Cor 12:12, 27; Eph 5:31–32; Col 1:18).

It stands to reason that to accomplish her mission of forming Christ in souls, the Church must possess the means to do so. And so she does, most notably the authority to teach Christ's truth and communicate His grace. The Church teaches authoritatively what to believe (doctrine) and how to live (morals). This authority, so often seen as a threat to human freedom, in fact answers the longings of the human heart. We all want to know what is true and to do what is right. Uncertainty, not a teaching authority, is the enemy of human freedom. As long as we are uncertain, we will not give ourselves generously. We remain enslaved in doubt. Confidence in the truth about Jesus and His narrow path frees us to run that path joyfully. The Church teaches authoritatively the truth that sets us free (see Jn 8:32).

But to know the truth is not enough. Since we remain weak and ignorant, we need Christ's grace to strengthen and enlighten us. Thus the Church administers the sacraments to her members, to bring them divine life, to nourish them, and to heal them when necessary. Or, better, we should say that Jesus *Himself* administers the sacraments, using the Church's ministers as His instruments. These means of grace, entrusted to the Church for the salvation of souls, have as their ultimate purpose the formation of Christ within us.

"Who do you say that I am?" (Mt 16:15; Mk 8:29; Lk 9:20). Jesus put this question to His Apostles, and it echoes throughout history. It is, in the end, the only question that matters. The Catholic Church exists, ultimately, as a living response to that question and to form the response in every soul: "You are the Christ, the Son of the living God" (Mt 16:16; cf. Mk 8:29; Lk 9:20).

The Church: Divine and Human

"[T]o what shall I compare this generation? It is like children sitting in the market places and calling to their playmates, 'We piped to you, and you did not dance; we wailed and you did not mourn'" (Mt 11:16–17). The Church always walks the same path as her divine Founder. Like Him she encounters those who accuse her of contradictory crimes and vices. They find her too worldly, and at the same time out of touch with "the real world". They insist that she stay out of politics and condemn her for supposed silence on issues. In short, the world demands that the Church be human and then complains that she is not divine. Thus in a roundabout way the Church's critics reveal the paradox of the Church: like our Lord, she is both human and divine.

That the Church is human is all too apparent. Of course, when most people talk about the Church being "human" they are referring to her failures (as if that is all it means to be human). But the human dimension of the Church continues in heaven, where there will be no failures. That the Church is human means primarily that she is built out of the living stones of individual human persons. She exists in the world in a human manner and through human means. She continues the presence of Christ by human words, actions, and relationships.

Unfortunately, since our human nature is fallen and wounded, the Church's human dimension also appears in weakness. This scandalizes as often as we expect to find purity and strength in the Church and encounter the opposite instead. And yet, as much as we ought to find holiness in the Church, it is in another sense not surprising that we encounter weakness. The crowds in Jerusalem encountered human weakness in our Lord—not, to be sure, moral weakness—but weakness nonetheless: the weakness of a Man betrayed, beaten, scourged, and crucified. The crowds looked and, seeing the Man of sorrows, in effect asked, "That? Is *that* God?" The Church always walks the path of her Founder. So people look upon the Body of Christ and, finding her laboring under human weakness, they ask, "That? Is *that* the Church of God?" Indeed, she is—appearing in human nature and laboring under human weakness, as did her Lord. And just as our reaction to the suffering Lord should be one of pity and not outrage, so also we should respond to His Body, the Church suffering from the scandals of human weakness.

Our outrage at scandals and weakness in the Church comes from the fact that the Church is more than merely human—and we sense that to be true. She is, as Catholics confess every Sunday, *holy*. This dimension of the Church is not as clear to us, just as Jesus' divinity was veiled by His humanity. We call the Church "holy" because she bears God's own life and grace. She teaches divine truths and administers the sacraments of salvation. Her very soul is the Spirit of God.

In a sense, it should not surprise us that the Church suffers (and always has suffered) scandals—not only because our Lord promised that it would happen (cf. Lk 17:1) but also because any human institution suffers them. What should surprise us is that the Church has survived her scandals. No other human institution could survive the scandals that the Church has seen. That she can survive them hints at the fact that she is more than merely human. Her weakness that endures testifies to something more than human at work within her. She is human, yes, with all the weakness that comes with that. But at once she is also divine, the Body of Christ.

Comfort with this paradox makes a heart truly Catholic. It enables us to trust in the Church as Christ's voice and presence in the world—the very oracle of God, as Blessed John Henry Newman said. It likewise enables us to see scandals in the Church for what they are. We can see the horror of a scandal, and yet not stop trusting the Church. We know the Church is at once divine—but also in need of reform. A person with such faith is not undone by scandals, because he knows the Church consists of weak human members (like himself). He knows that the Church is a pilgrim, en route to heaven, and always becoming more perfectly what she is.

Remember

They say the memory is the first to go. Well, that may or may not be true in the natural life. But it is certainly true in the supernatural life. Once we fail to remember the Lord and His works, our spiritual and moral life begins to founder. Thus Scripture is full of the commands "remember" and "do not forget." The Ten Commandments likewise begin, not with a commandment, but with a reminder: "I am the LORD your God" (Ex 20:2). After all, if we forget that truth, then we should not hope to keep the commandments.

The parable of the wicked tenants (Mt 21:33–41; Mk 12:1–12; Lk 20:9–18) presents Israel's tragic failure to remember. The parable's landowner represents God, and the vineyard he built is Jerusalem, or Israel in general. The tenants—Israel's leaders—failed to remember that He was the One Who made their vineyard. They had, as Isaiah warned, "forgotten the God of [their] salvation" (Is 17:10). Their forgetfulness caused them in turn to resent His commands. They beat and even killed His servants—that is, the prophets sent to remind them of God. The landowner's son—our Lord Himself—they killed outside the vineyard. He came into the world to collect the harvest but received instead the full brunt of their resentment.

We face the same danger as the wicked tenants: forgetfulness. When forgetfulness creeps in—when we forget that it is He Who made us and redeemed us—then we begin to view ourselves as independent from Him. We fall into a false sense of self-sufficiency. We grow to resent His commands as inconveniences, intrusions, and violations of our autonomy. His messengers become annoying to us, and we dismiss them, reject them, or persecute them. Unchecked, such resentment gradually becomes hatred for anything that threatens our independence—hatred even for our Lord Himself.

The Church constantly guards us against this forgetfulness. As a good Mother she forever reminds us of the Lord, His works, and His law. Although in our more childish moments we might regard it as nagging, she persistently says, in effect, "[T]ake heed lest you forget the LORD" (Deut 6:12). Through her priests and bishops she puts our Lord's teachings before us always. She points to what He has already accomplished, reminding us that it was He Who established us as

His vineyard. At the same time she looks to the future and makes us "remember" that moment when He will come again and gather His harvest.

Mother Church fulfills this apostolate to the memory most especially in the liturgy. In the cycle of the liturgical year she walks us through the life of Christ. Year after year she causes us to remember His Incarnation, birth, life, Passion, death, and Resurrection. We revisit His words and deeds over and over again. Furthermore, in the Mass she actually makes present our Lord's greatest work— His sacrifice on the Cross. She does not just recall or recollect His sacrifice. Rather, she makes His sacrifice truly present, so that we can conform our lives to it. And she does this in obedience to His own command: "Do this in remembrance of me" (Lk 22:19; 1 Cor 11:24).

If the memory is the first to go, it must also be the first to guard. Our Lord has established the Church as His continuing presence in the world. She is the constant reminder and living memory of Who He was and what He did. Let us then heed her teachings and follow her instructions, lest we fall into that dark and dangerous forgetfulness of God.

The Purpose of Peter's Privilege

For several months in 2013, after Benedict XVI's resignation and before Francis' election, the world focused on the papacy perhaps more than ever before. Unfortunately, most of the commentary and reporting tried to make sense of the papacy through the lens of worldly thinking—as a mere political position. Of course, for a proper understanding of the office we should listen not to the world, but to our Lord. Consider our Lord's words to Saint Peter at the Last Supper: "Simon, Simon, behold Satan has demanded to sift all of you like wheat, but I have prayed that your own faith may not fail; and once you have turned back, you must strengthen your brothers" (Lk 22:31–32, NABRE). We have here a nice shorthand description of the papacy and its purpose.

First, our Lord addresses Peter personally, using his given name: "Simon, Simon ..." But He speaks about a threat to all of the Apostles collectively ("all of you"). The fact that Jesus speaks these words to Peter individually indicates a special responsibility that Peter has for all the Apostles, all disciples—the entire Church. Peter must be personally attentive to the threat coming against them all.

Second, our Lord makes clear the urgency of the situation: "Satan has demanded to sift all of you like wheat." It is a terrifying image, speaking of the evil one's power—to treat us as casually as one treats wheat—and of the disunity and division he desires. To sift means to separate and divide, even to scatter. The devil seeks to do this to the Apostles—to scatter them, each one from the other. And he accomplishes this in the Garden of Gethsemane: "[T]hey all deserted him and fled" (Mk 14:50).

After this dire prophecy, Jesus then gives Peter a promise and a commission. First, the promise: "I have prayed that your own faith may not fail." We know that Peter's love failed, that he denied Jesus three times. But his faith enjoyed the promised protection of our Lord's prayers—for which reason he was able to repent and ask forgiveness. Again, our Lord singles out Peter for this privilege. But because every gift also brings a task, our Lord immediately gives the commission: "[O]nce you have turned back, you must strengthen your brothers." Peter's privileged faith is not for his own benefit but to be placed at the service of the Apostles, indeed of the entire Church.

This, then, is the lens through which we should view the office of the Pope. First, we take stock of the threats around us. The Church faces tremendous trials—martyrdom in Africa and Asia, political pressure in the United States, secularization throughout the world. Satan has indeed demanded to sift all of us like wheat. He wants to bring disunity and disintegration to the body of believers and likewise to sift us individually, introducing division and dissolution into each of us.

The papacy is established for just such times—because faith must endure and the brethren must be strengthened. The Pope is granted tremendous privilege and authority in the Church. He is the visible sign of unity, the head of the Church on earth. But his privileges are at the service of the brothers, of all the faithful. So let the world spin its wheels trying to get the real angle on supposed power politics.

We will pray for the fulfillment of our Lord's words: that our Holy Father's faith not fail, and that he strengthen the brethren.

Words Made Flesh

"Actions speak louder than words," we say, and, "He's all talk," phrases used to describe the man who says a lot and does nothing. Or simply, we may say, "Talk is cheap." These phrases from our culture all express the same basic point: words and actions must go together. They do not mean that words are useless. On the contrary, it is precisely because we believe words have importance that we fault those whose actions contradict what they say. We sense instinctively—on a natural, gut level—that the man whose words and actions do not match up is himself divided. He lacks the integrity necessary to be a genuine human person. He is not one man but two.

If such hypocrisy offends us on the natural level, how much more must it offend our Lord on the supernatural. Thus He himself declares, "Not everyone who says to me, 'Lord, Lord,' shall enter the kingdom of heaven, but he who does the will of my Father who is in heaven" (Mt 7:21). Our Lord does not intend to rob words of their significance but to emphasize that because our words are important they must be put into action. The faith we profess must be lived. Our words must become flesh.

Christ has not arbitrarily decided to deny celestial entrance to those who say one thing and do another. Such men deny themselves entrance because they lack the integrity of soul necessary for heaven. They not only lie but also make themselves into a lie; they are one thing in word and another in action. For this reason our Lord will say to such men, "I never knew you" (Mt 7:23). Of course, as God, our Lord knows them better than they know themselves. But, in a sense, He can never know them because as fundamentally divided men—as disintegrated men—they cannot really be known.

This demand for integrity of word and action helps explain the Church's rules, restrictions, and requirements. Mother Church wants to keep us from hypocrisy—to ensure that we live according to what we believe. In this regard, Pope Benedict observed that we Americans are particularly susceptible to a "separation of faith from life: living 'as if God did not exist' ".[3] John Paul II called this "practical atheism"[4]—professing the faith of the redeemed but not living as one redeemed. And the world longs to see in us this integrity of faith and action. How will the world believe in a Redeemer unless we live as a people redeemed?

Catholic worship likewise depends on such integrity, on the unity of interior devotion and exterior action. Our thoughts, words, and actions must be one in a common movement to God the Father— otherwise, our worship is empty. So Mother Church trains us in integrity of worship. In the Mass she unites our words and actions. As we make the sign of the cross, we say, "In the name of the Father, and of the Son, and of the Holy Spirit." As we say that we have sinned through our own fault, we strike our breasts. As we confess the Incarnation, we bow low. Our words become flesh. The liturgy's unity of word and action should characterize the entire Catholic life.

Likewise, Catholic morality is simply the living out of the faith we profess. Especially by works of charity we give flesh to the words "God is love" (1 Jn 4:16). And again, the world has a right to see such integrity in us. For this reason Pope Benedict called attention to "the scandal given by Catholics who promote an alleged right to abortion".[5] Such men and women are fundamentally divided, disintegrated people. They suffer the division not of mere sinners, who strive for virtue but fall short (again and again), but of hypocrites who consciously claim one thing and do another. Having divided word and action, they have divided themselves and present a false Catholicism to the world.

"And the Word became flesh and dwelt among us" (Jn 1:14). Our approach to God follows the same pattern as His approach to us. As

---

[3] "Apostolic Journey to the United States of America and Visit to the United Nations Organization Headquarters, Meeting with the Bishops of the United States of America: Responses of His Holiness Benedict XVI to the Questions Posed by the Bishops", National Shrine of the Immaculate Conception, Washington, D.C., April 16, 2008, no. 1, http://w2.vatican.va/content/benedict-xvi/en/speeches/2008/april/documents/hf_ben-xvi_spe_20080416_response-bishops.html.

[4] Pope John Paul II, General Audience, April 14, 1999, nos. 1–2, http://w2.vatican.va/content/john-paul-ii/en/audiences/1999/documents/hf_jp-ii_aud_14041999.html.

[5] "Visit to the United Nations: Responses to the Questions Posed by the Bishops", no. 1.

the Word became flesh to save us, so we attain salvation when our words become flesh in worship and daily living. As the world came to know God through the Word Made Flesh, so it continues to know Him through our words made flesh.

Lighting Up

We take light for granted. It is there for us at the flip of a switch, the press of a button. The night does not frighten us, because our homes and streets are well lit. But in ancient Israel it was a different matter. It was difficult to keep a lamp lit, even more so to find enough of them to dispel all the darkness in the house. And traveling, already a risky proposition, was virtually impossible at night.

"You are the light of the world," our Lord says of us, His Church (Mt 5:14). The image might lose its punch for us in an age of "light pollution". But its first hearers would have grasped its significance quickly, and we should try to do the same.

Light reveals what is true. Most of us have woken up at night and, in the shadows, confused a familiar object for something frightening. The bathrobe on the hook looks like a person; the shoe on the floor resembles a rodent. Walking across the room, we might stub a toe or bang a knee on the table we otherwise knew was there. By flipping the switch, however, we dispel the fright of the ominous bathrobe and menacing shoe; we avoid the assault of the stationary table.

So also the light of the Gospel reveals what is true about the world. Many cultures behave like us in a dark room. They labor under the darkness of ignorance about the world, about man, and about God. Nor do we need some remote tribe as an example. We ourselves, with all our advancements and artificial light, do not see the world clearly. We mistake ourselves as the masters, not the stewards. We do not see man clearly, confusing him for just another object in our disposable culture—to be used and dispatched as we see fit, rather than the summit of creation that he is. The Church sheds the light of the Gospel upon the world and reveals the truth.

The light of the Gospel is Christ Himself. By proclaiming Him, the Church makes known "to all in the house", not just to believers, the truth about man. As Pope Saint John Paul II never tired of repeating, Christ "fully reveals man to himself".[6] In a similar vein, Pope Blessed Paul VI described the Church as "an expert on humanity".[7] Like men in the dark fumbling for the light, we do not know what it means to be human.

Light provides guidance. Think of the headlights of your car. They are designed to show you the road, the path, to travel. Difficult to read by and terrible mood lighting, they do not serve any other purpose. So also the light of the Gospel is not for the stationary. It is meant for those who are on a journey. If we sit still with this light, it begins to lose its power and grandeur.

Light welcomes. In one of the greatest advertising taglines, Tom Bodett of Motel 6 pledges, "We'll leave the light on for you." We imagine arriving after a long journey to the warm glow of a lamp in the window promising security, warmth, and welcome. And this is precisely what the Gospel promises to the soul.

Light can be blinding. No one likes to be woken up by a bright light. It hurts our eyes and causes us to close them—as if we want to return to the darkness that had been so comfortable. So it is with the way the light of the Gospel is shone and received. The full force of it proves to be not a welcoming but a blinding light—too much for us all at once—and we close our eyes to it. Better for us to shine the light. The purpose, after all, is to enlighten—not to blind. We do better to provide the warm light of welcome and enlightenment than to shine the klieg lights of condemnation.

---

[6] Pope John Paul II, Encyclical Letter *Redemptor Hominis*, March 4, 1979, nos. 8, 10; quoting Vatican Council II, Pastoral Constitution on the Church in the Modern World, *Gaudium et Spes*, December 7, 1965, no. 22, http://w2.vatican.va/content/john-paul-ii/en/encyclicals/documents/hf_jp-ii_enc_04031979_redemptor-hominis.html#%241S.

[7] "Address of the Holy Father Paul XVI to the United Nations Organization", October 4, 1965, https://w2.vatican.va/content/paul-vi/en/speeches/1965/documents/hf_p-vi_spe_19651004_united-nations.html.

III

PARADOXES OF FAITH

The Tension and Balance of Catholic Teaching

Introduction

by Rev. Paul Check

"Whoever loses his life for my sake, he will save it" (Lk 9:24). Here is a summary of the gospel in eleven words. Jesus distills His saving doctrine into a paradox, and the most challenging of paradoxes. For what is more precious to me than my life? Who would dare to ask for what is most my own, for what will cost me everything? By what right does a carpenter from Nazareth, much of His own life veiled in mystery, ask me for mine?

This is the portfolio of Christianity: paradox and mystery. By paradox and mystery, the Catholic faith invites us to something—indeed, *Someone*—greater than ourselves, Whose very being is a paradox and a mystery: Jesus Christ, true God and true Man. The God of the New Testament took human form, died, rose from the dead, and now shares His divine life with us under the appearance of bread and wine. The Eucharist is the most precious of the paradoxes and mysteries of which Christ's Church is the steward, because it not only invites us out of ourselves, but it also actually *lifts us* out of ourselves.

Paradox and mystery stir the soul, and they stretch the imagination like a wineskin (cf. Lk 5:38). No matter what contentment or satisfaction I may feel in a given moment, and perhaps even in an

51

extended series of moments, my heart wants more than the goods of this world can provide. I want something that moth and rust cannot consume and that thieves cannot steal (cf. Mt 6:19). The soul longs for eternal treasure, even though eye has not seen, ear has not heard, nor has the heart conceived what this mysterious treasure is (cf. 1 Cor 2:9). Through paradox and mystery, we discover that what the senses and human experience cannot access by themselves remains no less real or wonderful or achievable. Through paradox, mystery, and the sacraments, we discover the One Who fulfills our hearts perfectly.

The Gospel suggests many paradoxes: joy and sorrow, faith and reason, obedience and freedom, suffering and peace, virginity and fecundity, and above all, a babe in the manger Who will hang on the Cross as an adult, but Who is the "Mighty God" (Is 9:6). Such things may not fold easily into the mind, but that does not make them irrational, or untrue. It makes them mysteries into which we are drawn.

G. K. Chesterton called paradox "truth standing on her head to get attention".[1] A paradox makes us pause, makes us think, and so it is an invitation to grace. Grappling with truth in an honest and thoughtful way is always good for the soul, and that effort will lead us to a loving Father eager for the attention of His children.

When the Father sent His Son into the world, the Incarnate Word was not "whittled down to human proportions", as Archbishop Fulton Sheen wrote. "Rather," he continued, "Christ was the life of God dwelling in human flesh."[2] Divinity in humanity, the supernatural in the natural, the eternal in the temporal, heaven on earth. The Incarnation recasts our way of seeing the world and so ourselves, by giving us a *sacramental imagination*, the power to see this life not from man's perspective but from God's. Such an imagination—a Catholic imagination—is not an escape from reality, but an embrace of it. And paradox is the idiom of this imagination.

How do we develop this faculty, and so better appreciate the value and purpose of paradox? Well, with whom do we most associate a vivid imagination? To little *children*, Jesus said, "belongs the kingdom

[1] G.K. Chesterton, *The Paradoxes of Mr. Pond* (1937; repr., Cornwall, U.K.: House of Stratus, 2008), 41.

[2] Fulton Sheen, "December 22", *Through the Year with Fulton Sheen*, ed. Henry Dietrich (San Francisco: Ignatius Press, 2003).

of God" (Lk 18:16). Cardinal Newman wrote that a child's "reverential spirit, looking at all things about him as wonderful, as tokens and types of the One Invisible, are all evidence of his being lately (as it were) a visitant to a higher state of things". The mind of a little child is a "blessed imitation", Newman said, "of what God will make us, if we surrender our hearts to the guidance of his Holy Spirit ... a foretaste of what will be fulfilled in heaven."[3]

Rev. Paul Check

[3] John Henry Newman, *Parochial and Plain Sermons* (San Francisco: Ignatius Press, 1997), 267.

A Faith of Paradoxes

More than one author has commented on the centrality of paradox in Catholic thought. One century ago, Robert Hugh Benson published his *Paradoxes of Catholicism*.[3] Later, the theologian Henri de Lubac wrote his *Paradoxes*[4]—and then *More Paradoxes*.[5] Along the same lines, but in a slightly different vein, Anthony Esolen has his *Ironies of Faith*.[6] G. K. Chesterton and, well before him, Saint Augustine loved to traffic in the wordplay that paradox enables.

The *Oxford American Dictionary* defines paradox as "a seemingly absurd or self-contradictory statement or proposition that when investigated or explained may prove to be well founded or true". Essential to the nature of a paradox is two things that seem to contradict one another but in fact exist in perfect union, harmony, and complementarity. For a paradox to work, there cannot be either one thing or another, nor even two things collapsed into one. Rather, two seemingly opposed things must be held in our minds at one and the same time without being in conflict, without one eliminating the other. A genuine paradox is not "*either* this *or* that" but "*both* this *and* that". Or, as Cardinal Ratzinger once observed, "A paradox is contrast and not contradiction."[7]

Now, Catholicism is a faith full of paradoxes. At every turn we reconcile seeming opposites and unite what appears to be contradictory. Catholic theology speaks less of "either/or" and more in terms of "both/and"—and precisely when others would see opposition and

---

[3] Robert Hugh Benson, *Paradoxes of Catholicism* (New York: Longmans Green, 1913).

[4] English edition: Henri de Lubac, *Paradoxes*, trans. Paule Simon and Sadie Kreilkamp (South Bend, Ind.: Fides Publishers, 1948); French edition: Henri de Lubac, *Paradoxes* (Paris: Editions du Livre, 1946).

[5] English edition: Henri de Lubac, *More Paradoxes*, trans. Avery Dulles (San Francisco: Ignatius Press, 2001); French edition: Henri de Lubac, *Autres paradoxes* (Namur: Culture et vérité, 1994).

[6] Anthony Esolen, *Ironies of Faith: The Laughter at the Heart of Christian Literature* (Wilmington, Del.: ISI Books, 2007).

[7] Congregation for the Doctrine of the Faith, "Message of His Eminence Card. Joseph Ratzinger to the Communion and Liberation (CL) Meeting at Rimini (24–30 August 2002)", http://www.vatican.va/roman_curia/congregations/cfaith/documents/rc_con_cfaith_doc _20020824_ratzinger-cl-rimini_en.html.

conflict: God is *both* One *and* Three, Jesus is *both* God *and* Man, Mary is *both* Virgin *and* Mother, the Savior is *both* Lamb *and* Shepherd, and so on.

The list could go on. The point is, we do well to appreciate the beauty and power of such paradoxes. Beauty, first of all, requires variety. You cannot have a beautiful painting with just one color or a beautiful song with just one note. At the same time, these diverse things must be in concert with one another. Paintings should not have warring colors and lines, nor should music have competing notes (which explains why so much modern art and music is ugly: it presents conflict, not harmony). Beauty demands different parts brought together harmoniously—complementarity, not competition. So in the Catholic faith we find different truths brought together in that harmonious whole called "the deposit of faith".

Second, there is the power of paradoxes to provoke. Their seeming absurdity (both God and Man? both Virgin and Mother?) ought not discourage or frustrate us. Rather, it should provoke a wonder and interest so that we pursue the truth more, and rejoice more in finding it. Like the parables of our Lord, Catholic paradoxes seem to be in the very nature of faith because they demand a child-like trust in God. They require us to trust that what *we see* as contradictory and absurd *He* brings into a wonderful unity and harmony of truth.

But the place of paradox in Catholic thought goes deeper than this. We can say that paradox characterizes—not just a doctrine here and there, and not even the highest dogmas—but in fact the very *pattern* of Catholic thought.

Consider, for example, the parables of our Lord. More than one of them delivers its lesson in a shocking, paradoxical manner that forces us to surrender our worldly way of thinking and submit to the Lord's. The tax collector goes home justified, not the Pharisee (Lk 18:9–14). The younger, dissolute son—not the older, obedient one—enjoys his father's blessing (Lk 15:11–15). The dishonest steward is commended (Lk 16:1–12), and the unjust judge is godlike (Lk 18:1–8).

Paradox is also essential to Catholic worship. At Mass most especially we find that God draws near, but remains far off. We find in the Church's prayer both great intimacy and transcendence. The sacred Host both reveals and conceals Him. Chesterton's paradoxical line from *The Man Who Was Thursday* summarizes well the liturgical vestments: "These disguises did not disguise, but reveal."[8] Ultimately, in the liturgy indeed we find *mystery*. And mystery rests on paradox.

Perhaps most importantly, paradox calls for a certain disposition in us in order to grasp it. It is something both reasonable and beyond our reach, and that can make us uncomfortable. Both Three and One; both God and Man; both Virgin and Mother—these paradoxes have been the occasions for many theological shipwrecks. And the pattern of heresy is always the same—discomfort with the mystery, discomfort with the paradox, wanting to solve it one way or another. Those who for the sake of ease try to eliminate the paradox, who try to smooth out all the seemingly rough spots of Catholicism, inevitably fall into doctrinal error. They reduce the Son to a mere creature, Jesus Christ to a mere man, and Mary to only a mother.

Paradox therefore calls for humility—indeed, docility, that willingness to be taught. Pride is to think that we can grasp all of reality and fit it into our minds. Humility is to recognize that reality is greater than what we can grasp or comprehend. Paradox resists the proud and lifts up the lowly.

Already and Not Yet

Every year it seems to get worse. The Christmas songs and decorations begin their commercial assault earlier and earlier. Now the yuletide ads began well before Thanksgiving. And there is no escape. The songs repeat themselves everywhere until the shopping mall sounds like one continuous DecktheRudolphSantaWeWishYou-Falalala. The decorations become more and more absurd, having less and less to do with Christ. Ironically, once Christmas actually arrives, these decorations and songs will be pushed aside to make room for the next marketable holiday. And on that day we Catholics will have only just begin our Christmas celebration. Until then, we

---

[8] Gilbert Keith Chesterton, *The Man Who Was Thursday* in *The Collected Works of G. K. Chesterton*, vol. 6 (San Francisco: Ignatius Press, 1991), 627.

must practice patience. We still have some spiritual preparation to go through. Although we *already* have it on our minds, Christmas has *not yet* arrived.

Already and not yet. This paradox of time characterizes the Catholic faith in general and the season of Advent in particular. We must preserve both together, not eliminating either one: *both* already *and* not yet. This paradox means, first, that Christ has already come and redeemed us. Even now we possess his life through the sacraments. He has already won the battle between good and evil. At the same time, however, we are not yet there. We can still fall away from His grace. We can render His victory meaningless for ourselves. Although we already have one foot in heaven, we must remain vigilant because we are not yet there.

This paradox helps us to understand Catholic worship as well. At one and the same time the Mass looks to the past (already) and the future (not yet). In the past we find our Lord's death and Resurrection, the saving events of our faith. In the future we look for "the blessed hope and the coming of our Savior, Jesus Christ". The Mass brings these two moments together in one celebration. It makes present our Lord's sacrifice as we await His return in glory. "For as often as you eat this bread and drink the chalice, you proclaim the Lord's death until he comes" (1 Cor 11:26). And that provides the template for all Catholic prayer. In our conversation with God we look to the past and thank Him for what He has already done—even as we look to the future and beg His help for what is not yet accomplished.

Hope rests on this union of "already and not yet". That essential virtue regards the fulfillment of a promise as both already accomplished and not yet fully realized. Hope fails if this paradox is eliminated in one direction or another. If we forget the already—that is, the promises Christ made and the graces He won for us—then we will not have any basis for hope and will fall into despair. If, on the other hand, we forget the not yet and foolishly conclude that Christ's promises require no cooperation or effort on our part, then we have become presumptuous and will face the Lord ill-prepared for eternity.

All of this helps us to understand Advent better, because it is a season about the past, the future, and the hope that they bring. As the Church's prayers during Advent make clear, we are looking in two directions: to the already and not yet. We recall our Lord's first coming to prepare better for His second. He came once in humility and meekness to save the world. He will come again in power and glory to judge the world. How we receive Him at his first coming determines how we will be received by Him at His second.

Body and Soul

"And they brought to him a man who was deaf and had an impediment in his speech; and they begged him to lay his hand upon him" (Mk 7:32). Without taking issue with how our Lord performs miracles, it is worth asking why He heals the way He does. "[T]aking him aside from the multitude privately, he put his fingers into his ears, and he spat and touched his tongue; and looking up to heaven, he sighed, and said to him 'Ephphatha,' that is, 'Be opened!' " (Mk 7:33–34).

Certainly the Son of God could heal this man without the gestures, groaning, and words. We know from other accounts that He could do so without even being present. Nevertheless, we can also presume that He has a good reason for doing it this particular way. Indeed, He does; because this healing—in all its physicality—corresponds better to human nature. Man is a composite of body and soul, an "embodied soul", as the philosophers put it. Our Lord could have healed the man by simply willing it. But He does it instead through words and actions as befits man's body-soul unity.

So much of Catholic life depends on this union of body and soul. There is no such thing as a "purely spiritual" relationship with God. The body is always involved. The sacraments, intended primarily for the soul, always use some matter—something we can see, touch, taste, smell, or hear. Catholic worship involves genuflecting, kneeling, making the sign of the cross, striking the breast, bowing—to conform the body to the soul and give the soul the assistance of the body. The entire person—body and soul—adores God. Our language indicates this also. The Church maintains Latin in the Mass for the same reason the Gospel preserves our Lord's healing word— "Ephphatha"—in the original: to communicate by the sense of hearing that something sacred is occurring.

The union of body and soul is the principle behind the Church's great tradition of sacred art. Fra Angelico, Michelangelo, Bernini, and Palestrina created great works not for museums and concert halls but for the soul. By means of sight and sound they hoped to communicate divine truths to the soul and to elicit sentiments of reverence and devotion.

As we all know, however, the body and the soul do not have the best relationship. They were created by God to be in harmony with one another. But through the sin of our first parents, we lost that original integrity of body and soul. They no longer work as one. Rather, the body rebels against the authority of the soul. And now the soul must discipline "Brother Ass", as Saint Francis called the body. Physical mortifications (fasting, abstinence, etc.) seek to train and perfect the body—not destroy it. The soul must deal with the body as a trainer deals with an animal, so that the body will obey the promptings of the soul rather than its own appetites.

There is a constant temptation to divide the body from the soul in worship. We easily recognize the hypocrisy of those who perform external acts of worship without any interior devotion. Our Lord justly condemns them. Perhaps more dangerous, however, are those who emphasize spiritual worship to the exclusion and even degradation of the body. Some of Christianity's most violent and destructive heresies disdained the body in pursuit of the purely spiritual. Such worship works for the angels because they are pure spirit. But for us, "Brother Ass" must be trained to worship as well.

The resurrection of the body will be the ultimate vindication of the body's dignity. Our bodies will share the eternal reward or punishment given to our souls. It is not enough, then, to seek the purely spiritual. You must, as Saint Paul says, "[G]lorify God in your body" (1 Cor 6:20).

Faith and Reason

At the crib of our Lord we find two groups of people not typically associated with one another: shepherds and magi. The shepherds represent a simple, humble faith; the magi—or wise men—represent human reason and learning. We do not usually lump such groups together, because the modern world has established an absolute separation between shepherds and magi—that is, between faith and reason. For the modern mind faith is intrinsically unreasonable, the essence of setting aside one's thought. And reason likewise proceeds on its own, with no need for any faith—that is, no need to trust in anything other than itself. The Catholic mind, however, ought to proceed according to the solution of Bethlehem, where shepherds and magi, faith and reason, adore happily together.

Even a cursory glance at history indicates that faith and reason can peacefully coexist. The two greatest philosophers in the world also happen to be saints, Augustine and Aquinas, as well as one of the most recent great popes, John Paul II; Benedict XVI was no slouch either. Also, many men of faith in the physical sciences—indeed many priests, such as Copernicus—contributed essential research and discoveries. The point here is not that these great minds also happened to believe. Rather, it is that such men made such great advances in the intellectual life, not despite their faith, but precisely *because* of it. Their faith was not some strange appendage to an otherwise reasonable life. Catholic doctrine provided the worldview and structure of reality that enabled their reason to take flight and in turn assist their faith. They possessed both reasonable faith and faithful reason.

More importantly, on the level of principle, faith and reason must remain united. Consider how reason depends on what we call *natural faith*. In order to think, I must trust a teaching authority. That authority might be an institution, a teacher, a book, or even just my own senses. Once I refuse to trust—that is, to have faith in—a teacher, then I have no capacity to learn and therefore no ability to think. If I do not trust my first grade teacher that A is A and B is B, then I will never learn to read and write. If I do not trust my science teacher that the earth orbits the sun and not vice versa, then I will never be able to think correctly about astronomy. And, as regards supernatural faith, if I do not trust the Church about the truths of revelation, then I will not be able to think clearly about God. Just as trust in our teachers years ago enabled us to think and learn, so our trust in God—our faith—enables us to know him.

Reason that refuses to have anything to do with faith cripples its ability to think. What has thrown modern thought into disarray is the rejection of any teaching authority. Such rejection is what Chesterton called the "thought that stops all thought".[9] It has gotten to the point that, as John Paul II observed in *Fides et Ratio*,[10] modern thinkers doubt their ability to know anything for certain.

Faith likewise depends on reason. Of course, the truths of faith are beyond (not contrary to) reason. We could not figure out the doctrines of the Trinity, the Incarnation, or the Eucharist on our own. Nevertheless, reason remains essential as both a preparation for faith and an instrument to deepen it. The human intellect can first prepare us for the act of faith by establishing its *reasonableness*—that is, that it is reasonable to believe and what is to be believed is not against being reasonable. Further, once we believe, our intellect not only may but (to the extent it can) *must* assist us in understanding what we believe. The history of theology is simply a rational reflection on the truths revealed to us by God. We can do this because we trust that the object of our faith, God, is reasonable and that our reason works.

The Blessed Virgin Mary displays this union of faith and reason most beautifully. When the angel Gabriel reveals to her the truth of our Lord's Incarnation, she asks, "How can this be?" (Lk 1:34). She has faith—she does not doubt—that it *can* be. But having that faith already, she then wants to understand more with her reason: *How* can this be? She would have gladly welcomed the curious combination of shepherds and wise men in Bethlehem. They are not at odds in her heart, but as one. In their adoration, the shepherds' simple faith is elevated to know the mysteries of God, and the wise men's reason is brought to fulfillment in beholding the Word Made Flesh.

Life through Death

Every culture and creed has struggled with the questions about life and death. What is the purpose of life? How should we live now?

---

[9] Gilbert Keith Chesterton, *Orthodoxy* in *The Collected Works of G. K. Chesterton*, vol. 1 (San Francisco: Ignatius Press, 1991), 236.

[10] See appendix 2, p. 185.

What happens after death? How are life and death related? The questions are so universal that people will often equate all religions by saying that they all have to do with "life after death". On the surface this may seem true, since every religion has some notion of the afterlife. But it does not withstand scrutiny.

Many, if not most, religions and philosophies resolve these questions in terms of either/or: *either* death *or* life. Or perhaps they simply set them beside each other as one after the other but not really related. The ancient pagans had a fairly dismal view of the hereafter: we are born *only* to die. The modern pagans have the opposite philosophy: don't worry, be happy—because everyone goes to heaven. Eastern religions, meanwhile, view the afterlife as not very lively at all. Their nirvana is not bliss but negation, the absorption of the individual person into some eternal being. Islam, while clearly professing a pleasurable afterlife, fails to relate deeply with death.

The Christian paradox reveals our faith's distinctiveness. It is not an either/or proposition but both/and: both death and life. Christianity, unlike all other religions, professes not so much life after death as life *through* death.

The Rosetta stone for this truth is contained in these words of our Lord: "Truly, truly, I say to you, unless a grain of wheat falls into the earth and dies, it remains alone; but if it dies, it bears much fruit" (Jn 12:24). It is not merely that the grain of wheat dies and later somehow wheat springs up. Rather, the dying is the very principle of the new life. It is through death, not merely after it, that new life comes. Within the dying is new life. Our Lord intended these words primarily as regards His own death. It is not merely that He died one day and rose on another. Rather, His dying and rising are intimately connected, mutually dependent. His Passion contains the seeds of His Resurrection, while His risen body maintains the wounds of His Crucifixion.

So it is for every follower of the Crucified and Risen One: the extent to which we die determines the extent of our rising. That is, the more deeply we unite ourselves with Christ in His Passion and death, the more we rise to newness of life. Whoever loses his life for Christ's sake will find it. Thus did Saint Paul express his entire mission: we are "always carrying in the body the death of Jesus, so that the life of Jesus may also be manifested in our bodies. For while we live we are always being given up to death for Jesus' sake, so that the life of Jesus may be manifested in our mortal flesh" (2 Cor 4:10–11). Our daily dying—in the form of sacrifices, mortifications, and selfless acts of charity—is the principle of our living a deeper intimacy with Christ.

Freedom and Obedience

Most people in our society (perhaps most of us) would agree with this proposition: "Freedom is the ability to do whatever you want." Such an understanding of freedom puts it at odds with obedience, which is, after all, to do the will of another. Thus, freedom and obedience end up in complete opposition to each other. And this is precisely how our culture views the matter: freedom demands shedding all obedience; conversely, obedience only enslaves those who embrace it.

The Catholic faith suggests something very different. The Catholic instinct has ever been to unite freedom and obedience (even if that has not always been happily accomplished). Our Lord himself speaks of both. He assures us, "[I]f the Son makes you free, you will be free indeed" (Jn 8:36). Yet He also says, "[H]e who does not obey the Son shall not see life" (Jn 3:36). And, most extraordinarily, "If you love me, you will keep my commandments" (Jn 14:15). These two lines of thought run throughout the letters of Saint Paul also. "For freedom Christ has set us free," he boldly proclaims (Gal 5:1). But he also speaks frequently of obedience (see Rom 1:5; 6:16; 2 Cor 9:13). For us, then, it is not *either* freedom *or* obedience—but *both*, together.

To grasp the relationship between obedience and freedom we should understand first that freedom is ordered toward the truth. Freedom is *not* the ability to do whatever we want. It is the ability to do what we are created to do, what we are supposed to do by our very nature. We are most free when we live perfectly the truth of who we are. Consider how a musician becomes a better musician (in a sense, *more free* as a musician) when he observes the truth about the music—when he plays, for example, Beethoven's *Moonlight Sonata* exactly as it is meant to be played. An athlete plays his game more perfectly—in a sense, more freely—when he observes the rules of the game. If a pianist flouts Beethoven's notes or a shortstop ignores the infield fly rule, they have not freed themselves at all. Indeed, they have enslaved themselves to their own caprice.

As in music and sports, so it is in the moral order. We exercise our human freedom when we live the full truth of our human nature. True freedom means obeying the truth of who we are, the truth of our being. It is not true freedom to disobey or reject our human nature—that is, to do things inhuman. Freedom, then, is *obedience* to the truth of who we are. And we have people and institutions in place to teach us the truth and to enable us to live such liberating obedience: parents, teachers, priests, bishops, and others.

The gravest threats to freedom, then, are not doctrines and rules but error and sin. Error—a failure to know what is true—prevents us from living the truth. And sin—the refusal to do what is true—is contrary to our human nature. It takes away from who we are; it violates our very purpose by disobeying the One Who has given us purpose. Of course, there *is* a form of obedience that is slavery—when we submit to what is not in accord with our human nature, when we obey what is not true. This kind of slavery exists not only in totalitarian regimes but also (perhaps more so) in the "free" world, where the mass of people slavishly heed what the majority presents as truth.

To set us free, our Lord gives us His truth to correct our errors and His grace to heal our sins. Further, He gives us the Church to continue His authoritative guidance. The Church's teachings, sacraments, and disciplines bring us freedom by giving us the truth and enabling us to live it. We of course must receive them with the desire to do not whatever we want, but what God has created us to do and to be. Specifically Christian freedom is the fullest obedience to who we are as children of God—that is, the full living out of that truth. When we respond in the proper way, then our Lord's words are fulfilled: "[Y]ou will know the truth, and the truth will make you free" (Jn 8:32).

The Paradox of God's Word

"[I]t has seemed good to the Holy Spirit and to us ..." (Acts 15:28). This verse, introducing the pronouncement of the Council of

Jerusalem (Acts 15:1–30) in a letter to the Gentile believers, is perhaps one of the most curious in Scripture. And one of the funniest: it sounds as though the Holy Spirit awaited or needed the approval of the Apostles. It is also an important verse, as it expresses the character of revelation. Like our Lord, revelation exists as a paradox. It is both human and divine: conveying divine truths in a human manner. And any attempt to "solve" this paradox, to separate or oppose these two dimensions, leads either to fundamentalism or modernism.

First of all, consider Scripture. At every Mass we hear the reading proclaimed as "the Word of the Lord". And our response—"Thanks be to God"—assents to that. It is indeed God's Word, His truth spoken to us. He is the author. But His Word comes to us through human means. God inspired the human authors to write in such a way that His Word takes flesh in their particular styles and genres. Their humanity is not an obstacle but a means of revelation. Just as the Word Made Flesh spoke and acted in a specific time and place, in a particular manner and style, so also the written Word of God carries the particularities of its human authors.

This means that the interpretation of Scripture can be somewhat tricky. In order to interpret accurately the divine truths, we must appreciate the human mode in which they arrive—the style, genre, vocabulary, setting, context, etc. But this human enfleshment also brings a great richness. Scripture is not just a flat recording of truths and events, nor is it a manual of doctrine and morals. Rather, we get to appreciate and enjoy the various styles of the authors. We have the details of Deuteronomy, the beauty of Solomon, the awe-inspiring (and confusing) imagery of Ezekiel, Luke's simplicity, John's lofty dialogues, Paul's powerful personality—and so on.

Contrast this with the Muslim understanding of revelation. Allah did not employ Mohammed's human intellect and will. Mohammed's style and personality do not show up at all. Instead, he was caught up in ecstasy and dictated word for word what he heard from the angel. He was not an author in any sense but merely a recorder. The human dimension has no place in Islamic revelation.

There is, of course, a Christian fundamentalism. It seeks to defend Scripture as the Word of God by insisting on a literal interpretation of everything—leaving little to no room for the human dimension. This does not work, because Scripture was not written to be read that way. Thus fundamentalism requires some serious mental gymnastics. It means insisting on an absurd interpretation of some verses ("[C]all no man your father" [Mt 23:9]) and denying the sane interpretation of others ("For my flesh is food indeed, and my blood is drink indeed" [Jn 6:55]).

On the other extreme we find those who insist on Scripture's human dimension to the exclusion of the divine. Although done to varying degrees, this always has the same result: the eventual reduction of the Bible to mere human opinion. It remains useful, to be sure, but only as another volume in the canon of religious literature. This modernist view has found hearing most especially in the mainline Protestant denominations, whose decline witness to its danger.

The divine and human dimension of revelation we find also in the Church's decrees. When the Church teaches doctrine, she communicates divine truths (the Trinity, the Incarnation, the Eucharist, etc.) in a human manner (councils, encyclicals, etc.). Some have a fundamentalist approach to Church teaching—not brooking any development of doctrine or diversity of language. Others see doctrines as, again, expressions of human religious sentiment. They are time-bound statements that "evolve" according to (surprise!) what the world thinks.

"[I]t has seemed good to the Holy Spirit and to us ..." Scripture and dogma reflect the divine/human paradox of our Lord Himself—evidence again that the Incarnation is more than one dogma among others. It is a paradigmatic truth of our faith. If we hold the paradox of the Incarnation in our minds and hearts, we will also hold other doctrines accurately and peaceably.

Joseph and the Paradox of Fatherhood

Saint Matthew's genealogy of our Lord ends with a real clunker. It begins clearly enough, giving a simple list of who fathered whom: "Abraham was the father of Isaac, and Isaac the father of Jacob, and Jacob the father of Judah and his brothers" (Mt 1:2). The list continues for fourteen verses. We encounter a few variations along the way, but the central phrase holds for forty-two generations—"Zerub'-babel the father of Abi'ud, and Abiud the father of Eli'akim, and Eliakim the father of A'zor" (v. 13)—until we reach Saint Joseph. We expect to hear, "Joseph was the father of ..." But instead we hear, "Joseph the husband of Mary, of whom Jesus was born, who is called Christ" (v. 16). Clunk. And this "clunk" wakes us up to the dignity of Saint Joseph.

Saint Joseph differs from all other men in the genealogy because he was not the father of Jesus in the same way that, for example, "Eli'-ud was the father of Elea'zar" (v. 15). His fatherhood is paradoxical. He was not biologically the father of Jesus. Nevertheless, our Lady and others referred to him as Christ's father without qualification (see Lk 2:48; 3:23; 4:22; Jn 1:45; 6:42). While not the father of our Lord in the natural order, he still held a father's authority and prerogatives—and exercised them faithfully. Paradoxically, Joseph reveals true fatherhood through the very fact that he is not a "true" father.

In our culture (as in most) the phrase "to father a child" means simply that a man performs the physical act and provides the biological matter necessary for a new human life. Colloquially the phrase describes nothing more than what an animal does (and also misses the distinction between animal "reproduction" and human "pro-creation"). Unfortunately, for many men in our society fatherhood begins and ends with the sexual act. Perhaps for such men a genuine term from the animal kingdom would be better: they do not "father" but "sire" children.

Some years ago then–Cardinal Ratzinger observed,

> Human fatherhood gives us an anticipation of what [God the Father] is. But when this fatherhood does not exist, when it is experienced only as a biological phenomenon, without its human and spiritual dimension, all statements about God the Father are empty. The crisis of fatherhood we are living today is an element, perhaps the most important, threatening man in his humanity.[11]

That is a strong statement from a man known to choose his words carefully. The paradox of Saint Joseph's fatherhood provides a remedy

---

[11] Cardinal Ratzinger, Address in Palermo, March 15, 2000.

to this crisis of fatherhood. Saint Joseph, precisely because his father-hood lacks the biological/physical dimension, calls our attention to the greater, deeper truth: that fatherhood is primarily and most importantly spiritual, not physical.

The Fatherhood of God, from which all fatherhood on earth is named (cf. Eph 3:14–15), is spiritual. In eternity, God is spiritually Father of the Son. This does not discount the extraordinary biolog-ical significance of a father, but it does prevent us from seeing that dimension as the most important. A man shows himself to be a father not by a mere biological fact, but by caring for, providing for, teach-ing, and forming the children entrusted to him—and, what is more, by doing so with a greater regard for their spiritual and eternal well-being than their material and temporal.

Thus we can say without hesitation that Saint Joseph truly "fathered" Jesus, because he fulfilled all fatherly obligations and exer-cised his fatherly role. In his human nature our Lord's character was formed. Then, as now, the most formative power in a boy's life was his father. So the Son of God, in a tremendous tribute to human fatherhood, entrusted Himself to the fatherly care and formation of Joseph. It fell to Joseph, therefore, to teach our Lord about the Cov-enant and the Law, to teach Him how to pray, how to work, how to serve others—in short, how to be a man.

Some writers have referred to Saint Joseph as the "Shadow of the Father".[12] This title means simply that Joseph represented God the Father. He stood in His place on earth. Although the title holds for Joseph in a unique and singular manner, every man who bears the title "father" is also called to follow suit—to be a "Shadow of the Father".

The Paradoxical Spirit

In his hymn *Splendor paternae gloriae*, Saint Ambrose exhorts us: "bibamus sobriam ebrietatem Spiritus" (let us drink the sober inebri-ation of the Spirit). That one phrase—"sober inebriation"—captures

---

[12] Andrew Doze, *Saint Joseph: Shadow of the Father* (New York: Alba House, 1992).

the paradoxical character of the Holy Spirit, Whose descent we celebrate at Pentecost. He brings us both sobriety and also intoxication. For the Spirit to breathe freely and effectively within us, we must accept both aspects of this paradox.

Pentecost manifests this reality. The Apostles' preaching amazes many. But others say, "They are filled with new wine" (Acts 2:13). Poor Saint Peter has to clear this up. Thus the first Pope's first public address begins inauspiciously, with a defense of their sobriety: "[T]hese men are not drunk, as you suppose, since it is only the third hour of the day" (Acts 2:15). And yet, in another sense, the Apostles *are* intoxicated. They suffer a certain inebriation that prompts them to act without concern for worldly honors, human respect, or even their own lives. They seem unreasonable and out of control in the world's estimation—as a drunk man would.

We encounter this inebriation in all those filled with the Spirit. They act and speak in a way that seems madness to the world. Thus the poverty of Saint Francis, the joy of Saint Philip Neri, the fidelity of Saint Thomas More—all are inscrutable to the world. We honor those men now. But the people of their time thought them mad. Even our Lord's friends say, "He is beside himself" (Mk 3:21). If the Spirit that consecrated Him animates us also, then we should not be surprised to receive a similar reaction.

At the same time, however, the Spirit imbues us with a sobriety—a sanity—that the world can neither give nor understand. "For the foolishness of God is wiser than men" (1 Cor 1:25). The Breath of God restores us to spiritual sanity by bringing order to disordered passions, docility to rebellious wills, and light to darkened intellects. Thus the martyrs, whose carelessness with their lives looked insane, amazed the world with peace and calmness before the executioners. Saint Thomas, whose rejection of wealth and privilege seemed folly, saw more clearly and deeply than any other thinker. Saint Catherine of Siena, whose missions appeared quixotic, attracted followers precisely because of her clarity.

Still today the Spirit-inebriated Church provides the world with remarkable lucidity of thought. According to Paul VI's words, she is an "expert in humanity".[13] The world despairs of any sense or

---

[13] Paul VI, Address to the United Nations, October 4, 1975, https://w2.vatican.va/content /paul-vi/en/speeches/1965/documents/hf_p-vi_spe_19651004_united-nations.html.

meaning to society, family, marriage, and sexuality. Our culture cannot articulate any coherent principle that would bring structure to society. And yet the Church, imbued by this reckless Spirit, presents the clear truth about man that alone brings order.

A familiar image of the Holy Spirit is the wind. On Pentecost Sunday "a sound came from heaven like the rush of a mighty wind, and it filled all the house where they were sitting" (Acts 2:2). Wind is an apt image, conveying what Saint Francis de Sales calls the "gentle violence" of the Holy Spirit.[14] Wind bursts into a room and upsets everything—throwing papers out of order, slamming doors, overturning things. At the same time, wind drives from a room what is rancid and stale, bringing a freshness and peace. The Holy Spirit— the wind, the Breath of God—accomplishes both in our souls. He upends our lives to get our attention, and cleanses us of the foul, fetid air of the world.

An authentic relationship with the Holy Spirit demands of us a willingness to receive both His inebriation and His sobriety. We must be willing to appear as the Apostles did—drunk, absurd. The unwillingness to look ridiculous places a limit on the Spirit's action. It says, "I will follow the Spirit's lead ... provided that I always come across as proper and acceptable." In effect, "I will respond to the Holy Spirit on my own terms." At the same time, we must surrender our excitable, mercurial souls to the Spirit's strong sobriety, which disciplines us from within, bringing order and therefore peace. For a new Pentecost to come, as it always must, let us drink of the sober inebriation of the Spirit.

[14] Francis de Sales, *Treatise on the Love of God*, trans. Henry Benedict Mackey (Westminster, Md.: The Newman Press, 1949), 87.

IV

THE SACRAMENTS

Christ's Life Placed within Us

Introduction

by Scott Hahn

"Sacraments bore me," I said to my friend. He was reading a book about the Protestant reformer John Calvin's view on Baptism and the Lord's Supper.

I was speaking honestly. In my mind, sacraments represented a "mechanical" way of approaching religion—ritualistic, mindless, heartless, bordering on superstitious. They were peripheral to most Protestant discussions of salvation and justification—the matters that really interested me.

"Sacraments bore me." Later, my wife, Kimberly, said to me, "Scott, I don't think it's safe to say that." She reminded me that Jesus Christ had established Baptism and the Lord's Supper. To dismiss these gifts was to flirt with ingratitude and maybe even blasphemy.

Kimberly's words shook me out of my complacency. Afterward, as I read the Bible, I was struck by certain details I had always glossed over. I noticed that God had a particular and characteristic way of dealing with His people down through the ages. He made covenants with them, and He always sealed those covenants, not with an abstract lecture on the nature of salvation, obligation, and Law—but with an outward sign, a physical sign. When God made His covenant with Noah, He set a rainbow in the sky as a "sign of the covenant" (Gen

9:12). When God made His covenant with Abraham, He instructed the patriarch to have "[e]very male among you ... circumcised" (Gen 17:10), again as a sign of the covenant. When God made His covenant with Moses, Moses extended it to the people by sprinkling them with the blood of sacrificial animals: "Behold the blood of the covenant which the LORD has made with you" (Ex 24:8).

These words and signs in the Old Testament would come to fulfillment in the New Testament. Jesus would speak of His saving work as a "new covenant in my blood" (Lk 22:20), and He would announce this at the moment He established the Sacrament of the Eucharist, or the "Lord's Supper", as we Presbyterians called it.

Moreover, Jesus spoke of the sacraments as essential to salvation. Of Baptism, He said, "[U]nless one is born of water and the Spirit, he cannot enter the kingdom of God" (Jn 3:5). Of the Eucharist, He said, "[U]nless you eat of the flesh of the Son of man and drink his blood, you have no life in you" (Jn 6:53).

The sacraments, then, were anything but boring. They were actions with ultimate consequences. They were matters of life and death, heaven and hell. God himself spoke of them only in the most dramatic of terms. Jesus' Apostles remained faithful to His example, and they too put matters starkly. Saint Paul warned that Christians who lacked proper reverence for the sacraments brought divine judgment upon themselves and were justly punished with illnesses and even death (see 1 Cor 11:29–30). Kimberly had good reason, then, to wonder about the safety of someone who belittled the sacraments, especially when that someone was an aspiring theologian— and her husband.

My newfound interest in the sacraments required constant feeding with books. I was building up, quite laboriously, to the doctrine that my Catholic contemporaries had learned in simple formulas in their religion classes. The *Baltimore Catechism* summed it up for American parishes a generation ago: "A sacrament is an outward sign instituted by Christ to give grace.... The sacraments receive their power to give grace from God, through the merits of Jesus Christ."[1]

---

[1] *Baltimore Catechism No. 2*, rev. ed. (Washington, D.C.: Confraternity of Christian Doctrine, 1941), part 3, lesson 23, answers to questions 304 and 306, respectively, http://www.catholicity.com/baltimore-catechism/lesson23.html.

Why did Jesus choose to communicate His salvation through signs? Because that is the way humans express themselves.

A sign is something used to represent something else. All words are signs, but words are not the only signs. A flag, for example, represents a country. Our respect for the flag does not arise from the value of the cloth. The honor we show the flag symbolizes our respect for the country. When protesters want to show their disrespect for a country, they often deface or destroy its flag.

A sign is a visible symbol of something that is invisible at the moment. We can see a flag, but we cannot see the entire country, much less the ideals embodied by the nation's government. The flag is the symbol of the country, its people, and its principles.

A sign reveals something about the object it represents. A United States flag shows, by its fifty stars, that there are fifty states in the union; the red stripes memorialize those who died in serving their country; the white stripes stand for purity; and so on.

Yet a sign also conceals much about the object it represents. For signs and things remain distinct. A flag is not a country; and even though we might spend years studying the flag, the nation itself will elude definition. The nation, in a sense, is a mysterious reality—a mystery.

A sacrament is like other signs, but also unlike them.

Like other signs, a sacrament signifies invisible realities, but its symbolic value is infinitely richer. Consider the Baptism of a baby. The infant is three times washed in water while a priest or deacon pronounces a blessing. The washing represents the forgiveness of sins. The triple immersion in water, moreover, symbolizes Christ's burial for three days; in Baptism, all Christians participate in Christ's saving death (cf. Rom 6:3). Yet the emergence from water also signifies the baby's resurrection with Christ—a new birth to divine life (see Tit 3:5).

And there is still more. Baptism evokes many scenes from the Bible, not least the Baptism of Jesus (Mk 1:9–11). The blessing of the water signifies the Spirit moving over the waters at the moment of creation (Gen 1:2). The washing is a sign of the cleansing waters of the great flood (Gen 7–9), the passing of Israel through the Red Sea (Ex 14:21–22), the river flowing through the heavenly Jerusalem (Rev 22:1), and much more.

Sacramental signs represent many realities, all at once—or at least a many-faceted divine reality.

But there is a more important way in which sacraments differ from other signs. For sacraments are symbols, but they are not merely symbols. They are symbols that convey the reality they signify.

All other signs remain distinct from the things they signify. Only sacraments bring about what they signify. Ordinary signs convey an idea about something. Sacramental signs convey the sacred reality itself.

There can be no more perfect communication than this. Only God could express Himself in this way. And He's trying to get through to you and me. No subject on earth could be less boring than the sacraments!

Scott Hahn

Baptism: Downward Trends

Why was Jesus baptized? Christians have asked this question for centuries. Sinless, He had no need to repent and therefore no need of John's "baptism of repentance" (Mk 1:4; Lk 3:3; Acts 13:24; cf. Mt 3:11). Likewise He has no need of Christian Baptism. As the Holy One of Israel, He has no sins to be washed away. As the eternal Son, the waters of rebirth are superfluous to Him. Even John the Baptist wonders at Jesus' approach for baptism. Trying to prevent Him, John says, "I need to be baptized by you, and do you come to me?" (Mt 3:14). Why then was He baptized?

To make sense of His Baptism, we need to situate it within the overall unity of our Lord's life. He more than anyone possessed unity of life. The various events, actions, and words of His life were not isolated and unconnected but united and coordinated. Specifically, they all find unity in His self-emptying for our salvation, descending to the depths in order to redeem us. His entire life has a downward trajectory, God descending in the Person of Christ to raise man from his misery.

With this descent in mind, we can come to some understanding of His Baptism by considering first its relation to His birth. This feast falls close to Christmas, to end the season. Our Lord's birth and Baptism were years apart, of course. But liturgically they are brought together, as bookends of Christmas, because they share a common purpose. And that commonality sheds light on the events at the Jordan. As Archbishop Fulton Sheen puts it, "The object of His Baptism was the same as the object of His Birth, to identify with sinful humanity."[2] In Bethlehem we encounter Him born as one of us. At the Jordan we encounter Him freely choosing to be identified with us sinners.

We understand His Baptism also in light of what lay ahead: His Passion and death. In response to John the Baptist's resistance, Jesus says, "Let it be so now; for thus it is fitting for us to fulfill all righteousness" (Mt 3:15). This "righteousness" is that right relationship between God and man that the Redeemer brings. We are restored to righteousness not by our own knowledge, not by our own efforts,

---

[2] Fulton Sheen, *Life of Christ* (New York: Image Doubleday, 1977), 57.

not even by John's baptism for repentance, but by Jesus' coming into the world and taking all sin upon Himself—by His submission to John in baptism. Our Lord's descent into the water expresses His assumption of our guilt and anticipates His death, burial, and descent into hell—the lowest point of that downward trajectory. The waters of the Jordan that covered Him have been described as a "liquid tomb", thus indicating the unity of His Baptism and His Passion.

So Jesus' Baptism is of a piece in the downward trend of the Incarnation. He descends to earth at His birth, and He keeps descending. From humble origins in Bethlehem, to ignominious exile in Egypt; from subordination to Joseph and Mary in Nazareth, to submission to John at the Jordan; from association with "tax collectors and sinners" (Mt 9:10; Mk 2:15; cf. Lk 5:29), to rejection by His own people; from crucifixion with common criminals, to burial in a stranger's tomb—His life is (to use J.R.R. Tolkien's line) a long defeat that ends in victory. It is one long descent that ends in the Ascension.

His Baptism of course prompts us to think of our own. Just as His was not an isolated event but set the trajectory of His public life, so also ours must bring unity and purpose to our entire life. Baptism is not only the beginning of Christian life but also the pattern of it. Yes, as we recite in the Nicene Creed, we believe in "one Baptism for the forgiveness of sins". But that does not mean that we leave our Baptism in the baptistery, any more than our Lord left His at the Jordan. Our dying and rising is constant and continual. Each day we die—to our selfish desires, to our pride, to the world's temptations—so that we can rise in being united with Him. Only if we are willing to descend into the waters with Him—not once but daily—will we be able to rise from them with Him as well.

Baptism: Heavens, Doves, and Voices

At your Baptism, did you notice the heavens opening? The Spirit of God descending like a dove? Perhaps a voice coming from the heavens? No, probably not. Even if you were old enough to know what was going on, you would not have noticed these things. Because they happened mystically. But they happened nonetheless.

At our Lord's Baptism these things did happen visibly and audibly: "[T]he heavens were opened and he saw the Spirit of God descending like a dove, and alighting on him; and behold, a voice from heaven, saying, 'This is my beloved Son, with whom I am well pleased'" (Mt 3:16–17; cf. Mk 1:10–11; Lk 3:21–22; Jn 1:32–34). These happened at our Lord's Baptism not because he needed instruction, but because we do. The heavens, the dove, the voice—these teach us about our own Baptisms.

First, "the heavens were opened". So also heaven was opened for each of us at Baptism. In fact, it is not until Baptism that heaven opened for us. As children of Adam, we are born in the state of Original Sin and deprived of the vision of God. We suffer the loss of heaven due to Adam's sin. Baptism makes us children of God and therefore able to enter heaven. Baptism, and Baptism alone, opens heaven for us.

What is more, Baptism opens heaven for us not only as a possibility but also as a right, as our proper inheritance. Just as children have a right to what their parents will leave them, so also the baptized have a right to what their heavenly Father gives them. The right to heaven, lost for us by Adam's sin, is restored to us by Baptism into Christ.

Second, at our Lord's Baptism he "saw the Spirit of God descending like a dove, and alighting on him". So also for us: at Baptism the Holy Spirit descended upon us and made His dwelling within us as His temples (cf. 1 Cor 6:19). Baptism initiates us into an interior relationship with God. In the Person of the Holy Spirit, God Himself now dwells within us as the "Soul of our souls", bringing us His gifts and virtues, directing our thoughts, words, and actions. From now on, the Holy Spirit intercedes not just for us but from within us (cf. Rom 8:15).

So why does He descend "like a dove"? The dove symbolizes peace between God and man. For Noah a dove signaled the end of the flood and the establishment of peace: sinful men had been washed away and God initiated a new covenant with man. Thus the Holy Spirit coming "like a dove" indicates that we who had been cut off from God by sin are now reconciled with Him by Baptism. Sin is washed away, and God establishes with us the new and everlasting Covenant.

Finally, at our Lord's Baptism "a voice came from the heavens, saying, 'This is my beloved Son, with whom I am well pleased.'" Baptism is the sacrament of rebirth. It makes us adopted children of God. But we should not think of that adoption in purely legal terms, as if it makes us "like" His children. God's adoption differs dramatically from adoption in this world. We are His children in more than just a legal or moral sense. By Baptism He places His life within us. We can truly call Him Father because we now share His divine nature.

In turn, He truly calls us His children—not merely creatures, not slaves or servants, but children. What a great source of consolation and confidence, to know that God looks upon us as His own children, with whom He is well pleased.

The Eucharist: Communion in Sacrifice

"The bread which I shall give for the life of the world is my flesh" (Jn 6:51). These words of our Lord admit of two complementary interpretations. First, we can understand Him to mean that His flesh is real food that brings nourishment (i.e., life) to the world. At the same time, these words have a sacrificial character. That He will give His flesh for the life of the world can refer also to His sacrifice on the Cross for the salvation of the world. Together these two interpretations bring out two essential aspects of the Eucharist: communion and sacrifice—or, perhaps better, communion in sacrifice.

True worship of God always has the character of sacrifice. Indeed, sacrifice is the highest form of adoration because it is the outward expression of our interior self-giving. By fasts, mortifications, prayers, tithes, etc., we offer God something to show our obedience to His supreme dominion and our total dependence on Him.

However, the sacrifices we offer God cannot praise and thank Him sufficiently. Because we are creatures, our sacrifices cannot rise to the level of divine worship. Our finite offerings cannot reach the infinite. And because we are sinners, our offerings can never be pure and unblemished.

So God Himself provides the necessary sacrifice. By becoming man and giving His life on the Cross, the Son of God has rendered the perfect sacrifice of obedience to the Father on our behalf. Further, in the Eucharist Christ has enabled us to participate in His sacrifice.

At Mass the sacrifice of Christ on the Cross is made present sacramentally under the form of bread and wine. It is no mere gesture of sacrifice or symbolic offering that ascends from the altar. The priest at Mass offers the entire Christ—Body, Blood, Soul, and Divinity—to God the Father. Because Christ is truly present in the Eucharist, the Mass is a true sacrifice.

Active participation at Mass therefore means that we unite our prayers, works, joys, sorrows, and sufferings—our very lives—with Christ's sacrifice to the Father. Joined to the Son's perfect sacrifice, our sacrifices become acceptable and pleasing to the Father. Further, by participating in the sacrifice of the Mass, we conform our lives to the greatest act of love and adoration. Notice how the secular world commemorates the birthdays and deeds of great men to keep in our minds the ideals and principles they represented. At Mass a similar but much greater thing happens: the People of God not only commemorate the sacrifice of Christ but also stand at the foot of the Cross with Mary and unite their lives with His offering.

But the Mass is a meal as well as a sacrifice. It is, as Saint Thomas wrote in *O Sacrum Convivium*—a sacred banquet. The sacredness of this meal flows directly from the sacrifice of the Mass. In fact, the Mass makes little sense as a meal if it is not primarily a sacrifice. Ancient Israel's sacred Passover meal was always preceded by the sacrifice of the lamb, whose roasted flesh they had to eat. The meal expressed their union with the sacrifice and therefore with God. So also in the sacrificial banquet of the Mass, in which "Christ, our Paschal Lamb, has been in sacrificed" (1 Cor 5:7), we consume the Lamb of God to deepen our union with His life-giving sacrifice.

"The bread which I shall give for the life of the world is my flesh." The Mass fulfills these words, because in the Mass Christ both continues His sacrifice to the Father for the life of the world and brings life to our souls by His Body and Blood.

The Eucharist: The Pledge of Glory

"Your fathers ate the manna in the wilderness, and they died" (Jn 6:49). Our Lord gives His Jewish listeners a stark reminder of their ancestors' fate. Those courageous men and women, the first Israelites, who came up out of Egypt, who passed through the Red Sea dryshod, who saw God's mighty works, who received the Law, who were miraculously fed with bread from heaven—they died.

His blunt words show the insufficiency of the manna in the desert. To be sure, the manna was miraculous. Every morning the wandering Israelites awoke to find that the Lord had again provided them with bread scattered upon the ground, sent from heaven to sustain them. They enjoyed a benefit unknown to any other nation: to be fed directly by God Himself. Yet as amazing as it was, the manna fed them for this life only. It was a material blessing and satisfied them for a time. In the end they died. For forty years they fed on bread from heaven only to hear, "[M]an does not live by bread alone" (Deut 8:3).

Our Lord gives this reminder to reveal the surpassing worth of the Eucharist: "I am the living bread which came down from heaven; if any one eats of this bread, he will live for ever" (Jn 6:51). The boast of the Israelites—the bread from heaven—pales in comparison to the gift of the Eucharist. Its insufficiency demonstrates the need for more than mere physical nourishment. Ultimately, that bread was for this world only. They died. The living Bread that we receive is the pledge of eternal life. Because of It, we will live forever.

Eternal life—that is the greatest effect of the Eucharist. Holy Communion brings to our souls the seed of eternal life and the power of the Resurrection. Under the appearance of bread and wine, the Lord brings into this passing world the everlasting gift of heaven. When a person nearing death receives Communion, we call it "Viaticum"— "food for the journey" from this world to the next. In fact, the Eucharist always has that purpose. It is the food necessary for the journey from earth to heaven. Indeed, it is the food of heaven already given to us on earth.

"Your fathers ate the manna in the wilderness, and they died." What will our descendants say about us? Will we be known as those who were nourished unto eternal life, or simply as those who died? Not unlike the Israelites in the desert, we Americans enjoy extraordinary material blessings. Granted, we must labor for our bread, as they did not. But is there now or has there ever been a nation so materially blessed as ours? We enjoy comforts, luxuries, and a standard of living that kings and emperors of the past only imagined. Even in recessions, our comfort and consumption seem little affected. Indeed, we lack so little that we risk viewing worldly goods as all we need.

All the more reason, then, for us to realize that no abundance of manna can bring us eternal life. "Your fathers ate the manna in the wilderness, and they died." If we trust in the manna of this world, we, like the Israelites so richly blessed, will die. Let us labor instead not "for the food which perishes, but for the food which endures to eternal life" (Jn 6:27).

The Eucharist: Abundant Insufficiency

"There is a lad here who has five barley loaves and two fish" (Jn 6:9). Thus we encounter an unsung hero of the Gospels—the boy who saved the day by offering a little bit of food. Perhaps he saw the hungry crowds. Perhaps he heard our Lord's testing question: "How are we to buy bread, so that these people may eat?" (Jn 6:5), and Philip's despondent response: "Two hundred denarii [days' wages] would not buy enough bread for each of them to get a little" (Jn 6:7). Whatever the case, he must have been thrilled (as only a boy could be) to race up to the grown men and offer his help. Imagine his excitement when our Lord—despite Andrew's grim verdict: "[B]ut what are they among so many?" (Jn 6:9)—used his little offering to work an enormous miracle.

The whole scene points toward the Eucharist. It happens near "the Passover, the feast of the Jews" (Jn 6:4)—that is, near the feast on which our Lord would later institute the Eucharist. It also follows the two-part structure of the Mass. As the crowds follow our Lord to hear and learn from Him, so we gather at Mass to hear Scripture readings and to learn (we hope) from the homily. Then, as our Lord takes the bread, gives thanks, and distributes it to the people, so the priest takes hosts, prays over them, and distributes them to the people. And between these two parts is the offertory: the boy brings loaves and fish to the Lord, and we bring bread and wine to the altar.

At Mass, as the bread and wine are brought to the altar and offered by the priest, Andrew's objection may pop into our minds: "[W]hat are they among so many?" That is, how can bread and wine possibly be worthy of God? How can they offer Him the worship He deserves? Of themselves, of course, they cannot. But we, like that boy, have placed them in the hands of Christ. Using the priest as His instrument, He changes the bread and wine into His Body and Blood, making them His perfect sacrifice to the Father.

Andrew's objection may haunt us again at Communion: "[W]hat are they among so many?" How can what looks like mere bread fulfill my spiritual needs? How can that small Host nourish my eternal soul? If it were mere bread, we would be right. Yet our Lord took ordinary bread and fed five thousand. And there was even some leftovers (see Jn 6:12). Likewise at Mass the same Lord takes ordinary bread and, through the ministry of the priest, changes it to His Body—more than enough to satisfy our souls.

The boy's offering and the offertory of Mass reveal the pattern of all offerings to God. We merely give Him what we can and leave the rest to Him. We trust that He will make an abundance of our insufficiency. The saints teach us this. When a generous soul offers what little he has, the Lord uses that small offering for tremendous good. Saint Benedict and Saint Francis, for example, sought to serve the Lord simply. Yet He took their offerings and used them to benefit the entire Church and the world. Saint Thérèse of Lisieux only wanted to live her "little way". But our Lord has used her offering to inspire millions. What seems small in the world's estimation—"[W]hat are they among so many?"—our Lord can make more than sufficient.

"There is a lad here who has five barley loaves and two fish." At your next Mass, imitate that boy. He did not withhold the little he had, nor was he ashamed to offer so little. Rather, he gave in confidence because he relied not on his sufficiency but on the Lord's grace. As the priest offers bread and wine, offer yourself in union with Christ—and from Him receive an abundance in return.

Confession: The Raising of Lazarus

"Unbind him, and let him go" (Jn 11:44). Our Lord's words after raising Lazarus should sound somewhat familiar to us. Familiar, not because we hear them often, but because they resemble other words we should hear often: "I absolve you from your sins . . ." To "absolve" means to set free—that is, to loose, unbind—untie. Our sins become chains that bind us in death, like the burial cloths of Lazarus. We also need to have them removed, to be untied. These similarities suggest that the entire account of Lazarus' raising provides a way of understanding the Sacrament of Penance. Indeed, we can find in the story the three necessary ingredients of a good confession.

First, sorrow. The story begins with great sadness. Martha and Mary and the Jews from Jerusalem all weep at the death of Lazarus. So the first step in a good confession is sorrow for our sins. Without this, nothing else matters. The crowds mourned the death of Lazarus. We should mourn the death of our souls, the death of Christ's life within us. The most significant sadness in the Gospel story is our Lord's. He wept at the tomb of Lazarus. Saint Augustine explains that our Lord weeps to teach us to weep for our sins: "Christ wept: let man weep for himself. For why did Christ weep but to teach men to weep?"[3] This is of course Gospel wisdom: "Blessed are those who mourn" (Mt 5:4).

Of course, penance does not require literal weeping. Tears are not obligatory. It does, however, require a sincere contrition for our sins—the rejection of them out of love of God, or at least out of fear of punishment. And with sorrow for sin must also come the resolution not to sin again. This is why the priest asks for the recitation of the Act of Contrition in the confessional—not to test you on the prayer but to ensure that you possess at least the minimum degree of contrition.

Second, confession. Our Lord asks, "Where have you laid him?" (Jn 11:34). Now, He knew full well where Lazarus was buried. He did not need them to show Him the tomb. But by asking this, He calls more trust and faith out of them. He wants them to show Him the place of death and hopelessness—where it hurts the most. And unless they take Him there, they will not witness His miracle. Notice that they do not say, "Go find it yourself." They say, "Sir, come and see" (Jn 11:34). They bring Life Himself to that place of death.

When we confess our sins, we in effect bring Jesus to our place of death, where life has been buried by sin. Yes, He knows our sins

---

[3] Saint Augustine, *In Iohannis evangelium tractatus*, 49, 19.

already—indeed, better than we do. By confessing our sins—by naming them in the sacrament—we hand them over to Him and give Him authority over them. We bring Jesus to the tomb of our souls—to that place of death called sin. "[C]ome and see," the people said to our Lord. By naming our sins—both the kind and the number for a mortal sin—we do likewise, giving Him authority to destroy the bonds of death within us.

Third, penance. It is our Lord alone Who raises Lazarus from the dead. But notice that for His power to realize its purpose, He enlists the cooperation of others. "Take away the stone," He commands them (Jn 11:39). And afterward He says, "Unbind him, and let him go." Consider how difficult these commands were to obey. Martha objects to the first command: "Lord, by this time there will be an odor" (Jn 11:39). And untying the until recently dead man was probably not very appealing either. Nevertheless, our Lord's divine work of raising Lazarus incorporates their human cooperation.

So also our acts of penance. God alone forgives sins through the ministry of the priest. He alone restores souls to life. But for His grace to work fruitfully in our souls, we need to cooperate. We need to do our penance. Thus the purpose of the penance is not to win forgiveness—God alone grants that, and freely—but to bring us into cooperation with the healing He desires for us. It is medicinal. The more we embrace our penances and perform them in faith, the more healing they bring us.

Our Lord did not raise all the dead as He did Lazarus. And even poor Lazarus died again. His miracle involves more than mere physical resuscitation. It points to that greater, spiritual reality we experience when we kneel in death and rise in hope.

The Priesthood: Missing the Mystery

A close friend from high school went to Paris during one of our school breaks. He came back enthused by what he saw at the Basilica of the Sacred Heart. Since he was not Catholic he did not understand what he encountered there. But that did not stop him from breathlessly describing everything: the architecture, the images, the candles, the incense ("A boy with a smoke machine!"). What really got my attention was his talk about a piece of bread that had become "some man's body". "Now, that's amazing," I thought. He handed me the brochure from the basilica, and I read it with great excitement. Then, to my shame, I was *disappointed* to learn that he was only talking about the Eucharist. Only.

That embarrassing exchange came to mind in light of reactions to the "mystery priest" news item several years ago. Now, there were a lot of things to like about this story. First and foremost the survival of Katie Lentz, the young woman trapped in her wrecked car. Her prospects did not look good until the priest came, prayed with her, and reassured her. Then there was the mystery of it all: Who was the priest? Where did he come from? Where did he go? When we encounter mysterious good works, we rightly intuit that God is near. Finally, for us priests there was the simple fact that this was a *favorable* report. It is nice to get one of those every now and then.

But now that the priest has come forward and acknowledged his role, we are tempted to disappointment. "Oh," we think, "just a priest." It was only a priest coming forward to help—praying, consoling, bringing hope, then humbly stepping back. Only. Not so miraculous after all.

We like miracles, but usually for the wrong reason. We chase after them because we think they will be the cure-all for our lack of faith. If I have a constant experience of the miraculous, then I will *have* to believe, right? In effect, we expect miracles to do the believing for us: "If God works a miracle in front of me, then I will believe." It is, of course, a form of putting God to the test. And the attitude fails to realize that many who saw miracles still did not believe. Every morning for forty years the Israelites woke up to the miraculous gift of the manna. But that miracle did not force faith on them. In fact, they grew tired of it. They failed to believe.

When God works miracles (and, yes, He still does), it *is* to help our faith—but *not* by doing the heavy lifting for us. Such extraordinary occurrences are intended to awaken our faith to the *ordinary* working of His grace. Our faith grows more when we believe the unseen than when we are forced to acknowledge the miraculous. Jesus brought health to the sick and sight to the blind—and people still did not believe in Him. He made the deaf hear and the mute speak—not so that we would expect that as a common occurrence but so that we would expect His grace to heal us spiritually.

We are like Naaman the Syrian. He wanted to be healed of his leprosy by a dramatic display of God's power (see 2 Kings 5:1–27). But his faith grew only when he set aside his desire for the dramatic and took a simple bath in the humble Jordan. And he was healed. Only when we trust in the ordinary and undramatic (water, oil, bread and wine, words spoken through a screen) will we grow in faith—and find healing.

So if the story of a supposedly mysterious priest grabs our attention, perhaps it is so that we can appreciate the *greater* mystery of the priesthood. That a man should come and go unnoticed might be remarkable. That a man possesses the sacred power to confect the Eucharist and absolve sins is truly extraordinary. God's glory is not found in a mysterious appearance and disappearance of a priest. It is found in the fact that He humbles Himself to use simple (and at times clumsy) men as His instruments of grace.

V

THE VIRGIN MARY

The Beauty and the Power
of the Mother of God

Introduction

by Lizz Lovett

A brown necklace with a picture of a lady on it—that is how I first met Mary. Before I met Jesus, I met her. She quietly crept into my life when I was about fifteen. A young man I had just met gave me this brown necklace with a picture of a lady on it and told me that she would protect me. I had no idea how that brown necklace was supposed to protect me, but I was a particularly superstitious girl and I tucked it away into my wallet. Every now and then, when I would dig through my wallet, the plastic holding the necklace would crinkle just enough to get my attention, and I would stare at it mysteriously and wonder who she was.

That gift of the brown necklace came at a time in my life when my parents' relationship started to deteriorate, and in turn, my relationship with my mother became difficult. I was a young, rebellious teen, and my mother was going through a difficult time in her marriage. If my parents weren't fighting with each other, I was fighting with my mom. When we spoke, we fought, and the only way I knew how to keep the peace between us was to keep quiet. So we barely spoke, and with that came distance.

During these years of my life, I had a good friend who had an amazing relationship with her mother. Anytime I would see them, they would always talk and laugh with one another. I would see them hug, hold hands, or just physically lean on each other. My heart yearned for that kind of emotional and physical contact. I wanted my mother to tell me she loved me. I wanted to be able to laugh with my mom, to hold her hand, and to tell her my worries and concerns.

I felt lost and completely disconnected from my family. I felt as if I was drifting day in and day out, trying not to feel anything, because the sadness of my heart was overwhelming. In a final act of desperation, I took the necklace and said, "Please help me." I hoped she would, whoever she was. My relationship with my mom stayed on the downward spiral until I left the house. I packed whatever I could fit into a suitcase and left to live with my older sister.

I kept that necklace in my wallet until my early twenties. I held it in my wallet for all those years, and then just as suddenly as it appeared in my life, it disappeared. Right after I lost the brown necklace, I started dating a young man named Ryan. This was the first man I dated who was a practicing Catholic. During my first visit to his house, he had icons all over his place, but it was the icon of Our Lady of Czestochowa that really struck me. Immediately I felt drawn to her. The beauty and sadness of it drew me in, and I would stare at it any chance I got. There was something about this lady that captivated me. I started to ask questions about her. Who was she? Why was she so sad? Who was the child in her arms? I knew nothing of Jesus and Mary.

Ryan took me to the gift shop at the Basilica of the National Shrine of the Immaculate Conception in Washington, D.C. He was searching for a gift for someone, and since I was in town, I tagged along. It was there that I discovered the brown scapular. I immediately made the connection that the brown necklace that I carried for years in my youth was really a scapular. I wanted to know more about the scapular and Mary, so on a whim I picked up Saint Louis de Montfort's book *True Devotion to Mary*.[1] I was hooked and started saying a daily Rosary within a week. My devotion to Mary felt so

---

[1] Louis de Montfort, *True Devotion to Mary: with Preparation for Total Consecration* (Charlotte, N.C.: Tan Classics, 2010).

natural to me. It was as if an old friend walked back into my life, and we were rediscovering each other. I had yet to believe in Jesus, but I knew that Mary was in my life to stay.

During the time of my conversion, my relationship with my mother began to heal. I was beginning to see my own sins and how they affected others, particularly my mother. I had held all of this resentment in my heart for her, and I never forgave her for one infraction. The weight of it all pressed heavily on my heart. I saw for the first time how my mother was struggling in her own life with her marriage to my father, the disappointment from her own parents that her marriage was failing, and the sadness that her family was falling apart. Just as Mary, the Mother of forgiveness, forgave us instantly for our part in the Crucifixion of her Son, I had to forgive my mother for all that had happened between us, and ask for her forgiveness too.

It's been ten years since my Baptism. The relationship between my mother and me is so much better than I could have imagined. While we still have a ways to go, we are working on deepening our under-standing and love for one another. Mary showed me how to forgive, and then to love, and that is what I am striving to do.

Mary continues to guide me as I travel through life. Last year, I was diagnosed with stage 4 kidney cancer, a diagnosis with no cure and a bleak prognosis. Being a married mother with four small chil-dren, you can imagine the panic that set in my heart at first. I begged Mary to guide me; to help me say yes as she did; to trust in the Lord and abandon myself in Him when I felt so lost and afraid. As tears fell from my face while saying the Rosary over and over, a spark of hope started to fill me. I anchored that hope in the Lord and said yes to the cross that was put before me.

Whatever may happen to me, I know and trust that it is the will of our Lord. When I decided to abandon myself fully like Mary, a deep grace-filled joy overcame me. I wake up being grateful for each day. When I look into my wallet and see my brown scapular, a smile comes across my face because I know she is with me, guiding me along the way and encouraging me to say yes every day. A brown necklace with a picture of our Lady on it—that is how Mary entered my life.

Lizz Lovett

The Paradox of Mary

Thus sings Saint Bernard of Clairvaux, the "Troubadour of Mary", in Dante Alighieri's *Paradiso,*

> Virgin Mother, daughter of your Son,
>   humbler and loftier past creation's measure,
>   the fulcrum of the everlasting plan,
> You are she who ennobled human nature
>   so highly, that its Maker did not scorn
>   to make Himself the Creature of His creature.

(canto 33, stanzas 1–2)

From its first words this imagined hymn captures the paradox of the Blessed Virgin Mary: Virgin and Mother, daughter of her own Son, humbler and loftier.

As both Virgin and Mother, our Lady reveals to us the dignity and complementarity of both vocations. Her perpetual virginity (i.e., before, during, and after the birth of her Son) serves as a sign of the pure, integral, and complete gift of herself to the Lord. From the earliest years of the Church, women have sought to imitate our Lady in this vocation, by foregoing marriage and giving themselves completely to our Lord, their consecrated virginity being an outward sign—a kind of sacrament—of their interior devotion.

Mary's motherhood in turn reveals the dignity of every woman who bears the lofty title of mother. That intimate and profound union of mother and child exists between Mary and God Himself. Every instinct, struggle, concern, passion, and love of a mother's heart toward her child exists in Mary's heart toward God Himself. And every affection that a man can have only for his mother God holds for Mary alone.

But it is neither that Mary remains a virgin despite being a mother, nor that she becomes a mother despite being a virgin. Rather, it is Mary's virginity itself that is fruitful. During the Christmas season the Church's liturgy celebrates that "the spotless virginity of Mary brought forth a savior to this world".[2] Her virginity became fruitful

---

[2] "Betaie Mariae intemerata Virginitis huic mundo edidit Salvatorem", *Roman Missal,* Roman Canon insert for Christmas; author's translation.

and fecund, bestowing on her also the dignity of motherhood and revealing that her motherhood is the working of God's grace. She is Mother of God through her virginity, the sign and expression of the pure and complete gift of herself to God.

Another paradox we find in Mary is that she is the daughter of her own Son. How can this be? This curious phrase in fact serves as the perfect response to those who say that Catholics elevate Mary above the need for her Son's grace. In fact, our Lady's Immaculate Conception and fullness of grace depend entirely—as do you and I—on our Lord's sacrifice on the Cross. By this sacrifice, our Lord won every grace for us. And so also for Mary. But He bestowed the graces upon her in anticipation of the Cross, and upon us afterward. The grace of her divine motherhood, then, is a fruit of her Son's sacrifice.

Finally, our Lady reveals the union and, again, the complementarity of humility and greatness. She, both humbler and loftier, is the first to live the truth that her own soul taught: "[W]hoever exalts himself will be humbled, and whoever humbles himself will be exalted" (Mt 23:12; cf. Mt 18:4; Lk 14:11; 18:14; 1 Pet 5:6). When Mary visits Elizabeth, she proclaims, in her Magnificat, that the Lord raised her up because He had looked on her *humility* (see Lk 1:48). His regard for her humility prompted Him to raise her higher than all others. This helps us understand the Immaculate Conception. Mary was kept sinless and entirely dependent on God so that He could fill her perfectly with His grace and exalt her above every other creature. So she became the first disciple of our Lord and the pattern of all holiness.

The Ear with Perfect Pitch

Any serious musician would treasure an ear with perfect pitch—that is, the ability to discern perfectly the accuracy of a musical note. Such a gift would enable him both to perform better and to enjoy music more deeply than most of us musical louts can. Being more sensitive to what a musical piece *should* be, he would rejoice more when it is *just so*.

At the same time, however, this gift would also be somewhat of a burden. Because, although the ear with perfect pitch better appreciates good music, it also more deeply suffers bad music. While most of us miss the occasional discordant note and go on happily enjoying a concert, the ear with perfect pitch winces and cringes at each error.

These same truths apply to our "spiritual hearing" and in turn help us understand our Lady. Our soul is created to "hear" the voice of God—that is, to respond properly to His initiatives and truths, to rejoice as we should and to weep as we should. But our spiritual hearing is flawed to one degree or another, by both Original Sin and our own particular sins. Our accumulated wounds and spiritual scar tissue make us hard of hearing.

Our Lady's hearing, however, has no such defect. She has the ear with perfect pitch. This comes by way of her Immaculate Conception: no sin ever touched her soul to warp her hearing. As a result, she enjoys the beauty of Jesus' voice, words, and message more deeply and profoundly than anyone else. No selfishness or pride ever distorted her hearing. She alone enjoys that perfect capacity.

But at the same time—and for the same reason—she also suffers more profoundly than anyone else. Every discordant note in the spiritual and moral order falls more harshly on her than on anyone else. Those spiritually and morally discordant notes that we do not even notice must have been like nails on a chalkboard for her.

We see the latter truth most clearly during our Lord's Passion, as Mary stands at the foot of the Cross. Because of her sinlessness, she suffers more than the others gathered there. Her innocence heightens her hearing. Her perfect capacity to receive our Lord's words and to interiorize His message makes her all the more vulnerable to the cruelty she witnesses and hears against her Son. Her Immaculate Conception, far from delivering her from suffering, actually intensifies it. The lash of the whip, the jeers of the crowd, the pounding of the nails, and the silence that fell when the tomb was closed—they all fell more harshly on her ears than on ours.

For the same reason our Lady also has a unique and unsurpassed joy in the Resurrection of her Son. No one else has ever heard the news of our Lord's Resurrection as clearly and deeply as our Lady. The words of the Risen One resound in her heart and soul without any resistance, with perfect clarity. Although the Gospels do not record it, the Church has traditionally believed that Jesus appeared first to His Mother. But this appearance was private, for Mary alone.

Imagine how her heart must have moved with joy when she heard that voice that she knew so well. Never have ears so gladly welcomed a voice. Never has a soul so perfectly embraced the good news of the Resurrection.

This is why we place ourselves in our Lady's care—so that we who do not hear so well can be guided by her ear with perfect pitch. She helps us to hear what our calloused ears cannot discern. Just as we stand with her at the Cross to learn its true sorrow, so we also remain with her (as the Apostles did) to learn the true joy of Easter. Our hearing does not suffice. For the angel's Easter proclamation to find the proper joyful response within us, we need ears better than our own. We need to go to our Lady and hear with her ears—and heart—that foundational Christian message: "He is not here; for he has risen, as he said" (Mt 28:6).

House to House

Our Lady had various reasons for hastening to visit Elizabeth. For starters, she could provide some much-needed assistance during the older woman's unexpected and probably difficult pregnancy. She would have been a great help, especially at John's birth. Furthermore, she made the journey to see for herself the sign the archangel Gabriel had given: "[Y]our kinswoman Elizabeth in her old age has also conceived a son; and this is the sixth month with her who was called barren" (Lk 1:36). The greatest reason for her visit, however, was not just to help out around the house or even to witness a miracle; it was to bring her interior life—the faith she carried in her heart and the Child she carried in her womb.

Consider Mary's faith first. As the Church Fathers were fond of saying, Mary conceived the Lord in her heart before she conceived Him in her womb. Her motherhood is first of all spiritual, a matter of faith. We venerate Mary primarily because of her trust in the Lord, not because of her physical motherhood. In her greeting, Elizabeth proclaims, "[B]lessed is she who believed" (Lk 1:45). And in Mary's own hymn of praise, she says not a word about her physical motherhood but points to her interior life: "My soul magnifies the Lord, and my spirit rejoices in God my Savior" (Lk 1:46-47).

That said, Mary had the unique privilege of bearing not only the spiritual fruit of her prayer, but also the physical presence of Jesus Christ, the Incarnate Word. "[B]lessed is the fruit of your womb," Elizabeth exclaims (Lk 1:42)—and we echo that daily. At the time of the Visitation God Himself dwelled within the Blessed Virgin Mary. Her physical presence brought His divine presence. It was the House of God who entered "the house of Zechariah" (Lk 1:40).

Of course, Mary houses our Lord, not as a building houses us, but in a most intimate manner. She is not just a dwelling place, but the person from whom He draws flesh, blood, and nourishment. Her body provides Him with a body: her blood becomes His, her flesh becomes His, her Immaculate Heart causes His Sacred Heart to beat. We rejoice that when we receive the Eucharist, our Lord nourishes us with His Body and Blood. At the time of the Visitation, however, Mary rejoiced that she nourished our Lord with her own body and blood.

To appreciate the Visitation even more, let us fast-forward to the end of Mary's earthly life. For the account of Mary's entrance into the house of Zechariah already hints at her entrance into heaven. Both the Visitation and the Assumption touch on the sanctity of Mary's body. There is in these two events a marvelous exchange: at the Visitation Mary provides her body as the Lord's dwelling place on earth; at the Assumption the Lord provides a dwelling place for her body in heaven. Given that He assumed His sacred humanity (body and soul) from Mary, how fitting it is that He assume her entirely (body and soul) into heaven. He brings His earthly dwelling into His celestial home. How fitting it is that the House of God be brought to God's house, that He assume into heaven the body from which He had assumed His body.

As always, what is true for Mary in a unique manner holds true for us as well: we are to house the Lord. We do so spiritually beginning at our Baptism, when the Trinity makes His dwelling within our souls. We house Him physically in the reception of the Eucharist, when our Lord makes His dwelling within us according to His Body, Blood, Soul, and Divinity. Our end will also bear a likeness to Mary's: to the extent that we provide a dwelling place for the Lord in this world, we will have "a building from God, a house not made with hands, eternal in the heavens" (2 Cor 5:1).

Assumed into Heaven

"Mary, the immaculate perpetually Virgin Mother of God, after the completion of her earthly life, was assumed body and soul into the glory of heaven."[3]

Scripture has no explicit mention of the Assumption. We can point to a prefigurement of it in the Old Testament: Solomon, son of David and king of Israel, enthrones his mother, Bathsheba, next to him as queen mother (1 Kings 2:19). This suggests the reasonableness and fittingness of Jesus, *the* Son of David and *the* King of Israel, likewise enthroning His Mother—and to do so He assumes her into heaven. This, while not a proof, demonstrates at least that Mary's Assumption fits within the system of salvation.

To understand this dogma better, we should situate it within the context of the other Marian dogmas. For Catholic doctrine is not a hodgepodge of teachings. It is a coherent, organic whole. All the doctrines form one body, each connected to the other. We understand one doctrine better when we view it in light of the others.

So, as regards our Lady's Assumption, we first consider it in light of her Immaculate Conception. We call to mind that Mary was preserved from the personal effects of Original Sin and was filled with grace. She was thus preserved from one of sin's gravest effects, the decay and corruption of the body after death.

Further, at the Annunciation our Lord *assumed* Mary's humanity to Himself, to become incarnate of her. She became the Mother of God because He assumed her humanity for the formation of His human nature. Thus, in a sense, the Assumption of Mary at the end of her earthly life is the logical consequence of His having assumed human nature from her at the beginning of His.

---

[3] Pius XII, Apostolic Constitution, *Munificentissimus Deus* (Defining the Dogma of the Assumption), November 1, 1950, no. 44, http://w2.vatican.va/content/pius-xii/en/apost _constitutions/documents/hf_p-xii_apc_19501101_munificentissimus-deus.html.

And yet, given all this, we still have the same question as before: What's the point? Why is this so significant that it needs an infallible definition? What does it have to do with us? Well, obviously, it calls attention to the importance of Mary's body. She—body and soul—was forever changed by becoming the Mother of God. She did not just carry Him for nine months and then part with Him. Rather, for nine months her body nourished His, formed His, and gave life to His. It is entirely reasonable, then, that the filial piety of our Lord would prompt Him to keep His Mother's body from decay and corruption.

What is more, the emphasis on the physical assumption of Mary emphasizes the significance of the human body in general and in the work of salvation in particular. All dogmas are timeless. But this one is timely as well. Our culture treats the body shamelessly. We are not at peace with our own bodies—hating them and worshipping them, treating them as playthings, viewing them as something we own rather than part of who we are: part of *us*. What Mary's Assumption calls to mind is that our bodies are made *for God*.

Ultimately, every Marian dogma reveals what God desires for each of us. She is the prototype, if you will. Her Immaculate Conception reveals that He desires each of us to be free from sin; her divine motherhood, that we conceive and bear Jesus spiritually; her perpetual virginity, that we hold the faith pure and undefiled; and her Assumption, that we be raised whole and entire—body and soul—to the glory of heaven.

Our Lady of Promptness

The Virgin Mary bears many titles and is invoked by many names. In his 2014 Chrism Mass homily, Pope Francis gave us a new one to consider: Our Lady of Promptness. A quick Internet search for this title brings up only references to the same homily. So it would seem that the title is the Pope's own creation. But as is so often the case with Pope Francis, this novelty has deep roots in the Catholic faith.

The Pope takes his inspiration from the account of the Visitation: "In those days Mary arose and went with haste into the hill country, to a city of Judah" (Lk 1:39). The crucial words here are "with haste" ("in haste" or "with all haste" in other translations). Of course, "haste" does not always have good connotations in our culture. "Haste makes waste," we perhaps heard as children. Pope Francis refers to the original Greek for this term: *meta spoude*—which can certainly be "with haste". But it could also be translated "with diligence" or, as the Pope takes it, "with promptness", *promptly*.

In her response to the news about Elizabeth, Mary is not rushed or harried, but prompt and diligent. No sooner does the archangel Gabriel depart from her than she sets out—in haste, with diligence, *promptly*—to visit Elizabeth. She makes this visit certainly to assist the older woman during what would have been a difficult pregnancy and first months with her son. But she visits Elizabeth primarily to encounter the sign promised by Gabriel: "[B]ehold, your kinswoman Elizabeth in her old age has also conceived a son; and this is the sixth month with her who was called barren. For with God nothing will be impossible" (Lk 1:36–37).

In short, Mary is prompt about the things of God. In this we find her again to be *the* example of the Christian life. She does not delay or put things off. She responds immediately and generously. Her purity of heart brings about a singularity of purpose. She is not distracted by competing loves, not interiorly divided, not hesitant in her commitment. Her promptness anticipates her own Son's powerful and shocking exhortation to discipleship: "Follow me, and leave the dead to bury their own dead" (Mt 8:22).

As always, Mary demonstrates in a singular way what is true for all Christians. Those imbued with the life of Christ respond promptly to His initiatives, to His every last suggestion. Indeed, the goal of the Christian life is to become receptive and immediately responsive to God's action within us. We must therefore cultivate the diligence and promptness exemplified by Mary.

And it is precisely the *lack* of such promptness that enmeshes us in sin. Most of us sin, not out of malice or hatred, but out of slowness and negligence, by putting things off. We delay about the things of God and thus create room for lesser loves and lesser goods to distract and overwhelm us. We violate the Sabbath not because we hate the Mass but because we fail to make it a priority. We allow other things—soccer, vacations, errands—to distract us. And if that continues, we soon will resent the Mass. Likewise we fail to pray because we simply do not act as promptly as we should. God's initiative is there—but we put off our response, often failing to give it at all. And how many good works do we omit, not deliberately, but because we delay and procrastinate and eventually set them aside altogether?

The word "diligence" comes from *diligo*, the Latin for "love". We are diligent about what we love. When a man loves sports, he is swift to check the schedules, scores, and stats. When a man loves a woman, he occupies himself with knowing her better and doing what pleases her. And when we love God, we are attentive and responsive to His every touch—no matter how slight—to knowing and doing what pleases Him.

Dante Alighieri never heard the title "Our Lady of Promptness". But he would have appreciated it immediately. In his *Purgatorio*, souls are purged of sloth—that slowness and lassitude about the things of God—by racing around the mountain while repeating, "Mary ran to the hill country in haste!"[4] Dante understood that our Lady's example of promptness is the cure for our sluggishness.

As her kinswoman Elizabeth learned, Mary's promptness to the things of God necessarily involves her care for others. She visited Elizabeth to see God's sign, to assist her relative, but also to bring the presence of the Child in her womb. We also benefit from this swift solicitude. She is Our Lady of Promptness also in her care for us. She knows better than anyone else God's loves for us and His desire for our salvation. For this reason she does not delay in answering our prayers. She comes with haste to help us by her example, her intercession, and her maternal care.

Virgin Most Powerful

As Catholics approach Christmas, we hear and read many prophecies about our Lord coming in *power*. They announce seismic changes: valleys filled in, mountains and hills brought low, rugged lands made

---

[4] Dante Alighieri, *Purgatorio*, canto 18, 100, in *Purgatory*, trans. Anthony Esolen (New York: The Modern Library, 2003), 197.

plain, and rough countries turned into broad valleys (see Is 40:4). We hear about the One Who "shall judge between the nations, and shall decide for many peoples" (Is 2:4). He comes with vindication (cf. Is 35:4). "Behold, the LORD God comes with might, and his arm rules for him" (Is 40:10).

But when He does arrive, it is not as we expect. It is so different, in fact, that we might be tempted to think that prophecies of His powerful coming were wrong. But it is we who are wrong—about the nature of true power. We associate power with volume and size. The louder and bigger, the more powerful. Our Lord comes instead in a hidden, simple, small, quiet—indeed, silent—manner. And yet He comes to us by way of the one we invoke as "Virgin Most Powerful".

Simply to call the Virgin Mary powerful seems odd enough. After all, she was *least powerful* in her culture. She was young, childless, and female—none of which gained her any standing or authority in that society. So when the archangel appeared and saluted her as "full of grace" (Lk 1:28), he was speaking to someone powerless in the world's estimation. And the moment she conceived, she became—if possible—even more powerless. For her untimely pregnancy exposed her to accusations of adultery and to the punishment for that sin: death.

Still, we invoke her as "Virgin Most Powerful"—because our Lady reveals where true power lies. We associate her with silence, smallness, and purity. It is through these that the omnipotent God first entered the world. And it is through these that He comes again.

First, silence. We think power is in volume. We shout to make our point; we blast radios to announce our coming. In contrast, our Lady possesses a deeper, genuine power in her silence. Despite the angelic choirs and the shepherds coming on the scene, we rightly sense that our Lord's birth was characterized by silence. As Christmas carols inform us, the night is silent and, on account of the sleeping Baby, we must be still, still, still. Saint Luke is the first lyricist: "Mary kept all these things, pondering them in her heart" (Lk 2:19). We find her not speaking, not making any noise, but reflecting, meditating in the silence of Bethlehem.

Silence speaks. It points us to mysteries that human words cannot encompass or communicate. In the presence of glory and majesty, we shut our mouths. And in the presence of love, lovers do not need to speak: their silent presence to one another communicates enough. Scripture tells us not only of heaven's music, but also of its equally important silence (see Rev 8:1). When the excited shepherds, fresh from an angelic concert, arrive at the stable, they encounter the silence of Mary—a silence that points them to the mystery in the manger. Before the Word Made Flesh we realize the insufficiency of our words.

Second, smallness. Again, we associate power with what is big and large. We may not like bullies, but we buy into their way of thinking: might makes right. The bigger the better. But God works differently. He exalts little Israel over great Egypt, Gideon over the Midianites, and David over Goliath. With Mary the Lord of Hosts begins the definitive victory of the small over the great.

Mary is small in the sense of being insignificant, possessing no power, no authority—indeed, not even being known. She lived in a small village in a no-account area of a vast empire. Nevertheless, the Lord looked upon Mary, and specifically upon her "low estate" (Lk 1:48), *humility*, and *lowliness*. It was precisely her smallness that attracted Him. So her smallness points to another smallness—a greater smallness, if you will: the smallness of God. It was by means of Mary's humility—that powerful spiritual littleness—that God became small Himself, the smallest life in the womb, the Babe in the manger. Her willingness to be small made room for the Almighty to be small.

Third, purity. The world tends to associate power with sex. Men have long identified power with sexual conquests. Power, as the saying goes, is the greatest aphrodisiac. Thanks to the sexual license of our culture, women are now "free" to embrace the same delusion. The freedom to be sexually impure is at the heart of our culture's view of power. Virginity thus appears as a deprivation rather than a fullness, weakness rather than power.

Virginity was not prized in ancient Israel either—not for libidinous reasons, but because a virgin could not be the mother of the Messiah, which was the desire of devout Jewish women. So Mary's virginity makes her appear even more powerless.

But as both Virgin and Mother, Mary in fact manifests *the power of purity*. It is not merely that she becomes a mother while remaining a virgin. Rather, the absolute spiritual and physical self-gift Mary makes by her virginity becomes the means by which salvation enters the world.

What is true for Mary in an exceptional way holds true for all of us more broadly: purity confers a certain life-giving power. It is the power to give oneself because purity is the full possession of oneself. It also brings the ability to see and to know. The mind is cleared of the desires that fog thinking. "Blessed are the pure in heart, for they shall see God" (Mt 5:8).

In all these things our Lady shows us true power—the power of grace that comes to us always in silence, smallness, and purity. It is a power not of our own making or control. It is God's work within us, as it was exceptionally within Mary. We cannot demand or force the working of grace. We must, rather, wait—silently, humbly, and of pure of heart.

Needing to Be Proclaimed

The Litany of the Blessed Virgin Mary invokes our Lady as "Virgin most renowned". It is of course a fair description—most renowned because she alone is both Virgin and Mother; most renowned because through her virginity she became the Mother of God; most renowned as she herself foretold: "For behold, henceforth all generations will call me blessed" (Lk 1:48).

Virgin most renowned. The Latin for this invocation brings out another dimension: *Virgo praedicanda*—literally, "Virgin needing to be proclaimed"—not that she is not already known and renowned, but that she still needs to be made known. And this is so for one simple reason: Mary is the full flowering of the grace of Jesus Christ. To know her is to know what He has accomplished, what His victory has won. She, the perfection of grace, shows in a singular manner what all of us are called to become. Mary embodies her Son's every teaching and instruction—and therefore all preaching. In proclaiming her, we in effect proclaim the fullness of the Gospel.

Consider this first as regards our Lord's proclamation of the Gospel. We do not know how often our Lady heard her Son preach. Perhaps she was there in the crowd, listening peacefully. Nevertheless, whether physically or in His mind's eye, she was present as He taught. In her He had before Him the perfection, the fullness of what He preached. In a sense by preaching the Gospel, He was proclaiming her who is "full of grace". And her presence must have brought Him great consolation as others rejected Him. When the crowds turned on Him, Mary stood by Him. And by her holiness she witnessed to the truth they rejected. Most especially in His most important pulpit, the Cross, He drew comfort and encouragement from the very sight of Mary—the living vindication of all He taught and accomplished—His victory already present.

As for our Lord's ministry, so also for that of His Church. Mary needs to be proclaimed as the full flowering of Gospel grace and truth. We may draw back from speaking about her, not wanting to offend or come across as odd and overdevotional. But the Christian life cannot be understood apart from her, for she is the only human person to be perfectly defined by the grace of Christ.

We preach and proclaim the Virgin Mary first of all because she simply deserves it. We do not remain silent about truths. And the more glorious a truth, the more we proclaim it. In Mary we find the glorious truth that God created one of us (Mary is not superhuman but fully human) without sin—that He became her Son, was carried in her womb, rested in her lap, obeyed her words, and was entombed by her hands; that He made her fruitful, becoming man not despite her virginity but through it; and that He assumed her body and soul to Himself, not allowing the power of death to corrupt even her body.

But notice that in such preaching about Mary, in making known what God has accomplished in her, we also proclaim something about ourselves. For every dogma about our Lady applies in a certain way to us as well. She is the realization of all that He has promised us. The singular graces she received reveal what God intends to accomplish for all. She reveals to us what it means to be a disciple of Christ. In the truth about her we find our calling.

By keeping her free from sin He shows that He desires to deliver all of us from sin and make us full of grace—*defined* by grace, as she was. In her becoming the Mother of God, we learn that He desires us to conceive Him in our thoughts and bring Him forth by our words and actions. "For whoever does the will of my Father in heaven is my brother, and sister, and *mother*" (Mt 12:50; italics added). He makes her virginity fruitful because He intends our souls likewise to be pure and fruitful. And He assumes her body and soul into heaven because He desires to raise our bodies to the same glory.

In proclaiming Mary we make known not only Christ's master-piece of grace but also what He desires to accomplish in us. She, the Church in her perfection, needs to be proclaimed and preached so that the truth of Christ's victory and grace will shine forth more clearly.

VI

THE SAINTS

The Mortal Masterpieces of God's Grace

Introduction

by Mary Ellen Bork

One of the blessings of being a Catholic is discovering we are part of a large extended family of holy people. Their stories cover many centuries and diverse cultures, and knowing them, we come to a better understanding of Christ, the One they loved and followed. We all entered this family through Baptism into Christ, and those who have gone before us have invaluable lessons to teach about how to love Christ and serve Him, even in difficult circumstances. In the liturgy the Church continually remembers their holy lives, holding them up for our meditation and imitation. But they are not just models on pedestals for us to look at. They are with Christ in heaven and care about us as we make our way to heaven. Through the Eucharist, we are in communion with them and they are praying for us. Saint Thérèse, the Little Flower, famously said, "I want to spend my heaven in doing good on earth."[1] Not to know a few of these saints is to miss part of the great treasure of our Catholic heritage.

The special role of saints, a bit like our guardian angels, is to inspire us to go the extra mile, to take the risky step we might not have

---

[1] Saint Thérèse of Lisieux, *The Final Conversations*, trans. John Clarke (Washington, D.C.: ICS, 1977), 102.

thought we were capable of, to go forward in faith beyond what is conventional, to love deeply so as not to be just a clanging symbol. Who does not need that constant reminder in an age of distracted self-centeredness?

I have come to admire and love Saint Catherine of Siena, an extraordinary woman, called to live a deep life of prayer and remain in the world, instead of the more customary choice of convent life in fourteenth-century Italy. It was a time of constant warfare between cities and families with all the uncertainty and suffering that constant upheaval brings. Terror reigned in the streets. She confronted the forces of disintegration with her personal witness to the power of love. She convinced the Pope to return to Rome from Avignon and helped restore unity in the Church. She quoted Christ as saying to her, "You harm your neighbors by not giving them the pleasure of the love and charity you owe them."[2] Everyone has gifts that others need to grow in faith and love, and we are meant to share them, not hold on to them or hide them, or let them gather dust from disuse.

Saint Catherine became very real for me when, in 2014, I was asked to prepare a talk on her for a pilgrimage to Central Italy with the John Carroll Society, a group of Catholic laypeople. The talk was to be given in Siena, where she was born and lived. In the course of reading her dialogues and discussing them with knowledgeable friends, I was struck with an awe of her that put a distance between Catherine and me. Slowly that distance began to fade as it became clear to me that the quality that attracted her many followers was her loving attentiveness to tout for sightseeing. The introduction to her life oriented our visit. I felt Catherine helped me prepare my remarks, and she has remained with me ever since that visit, always encouraging me to grow in the love of God. She was a mystic, a diplomat, and a spiritual leader, but a witness to love first. We arrived in Siena, and I gave my talk early in the morning before we started.

Another favorite of mine is Saint Thomas More, the English chancellor to Henry VIII. Thomas was an outstanding legal mind, loving father, and writer who had to disagree with the king on the question of dissolving his marriage to his queen, Catherine, in order to marry

[2] Catherine of Siena, *Catherine of Siena: The Dialogue*, trans. and introduction by Suzanne Noffke, O.P., Classics of Western Spirituality (New York: Paulist Press, 1980), 34.

Anne Boleyn. Thomas suffered the loss of everything—his position, possessions, and even his life—for the sake of truth and defense of marriage. This did not make him sad but rather made him trust the Lord completely and look forward to being with Him in heaven. His friend Bishop John Fisher, as an official of the Church, had to tell Henry that divorcing his wife was wrong. He too suffered imprisonment and death in witness to the truth. John Fisher knew that heaven was more important than trying to impress or placate the king by acquiescing to his marital desires.

Saint Thomas More has a special place in my family. My husband, Robert, was a constitutional lawyer and a federal judge. When I was president of the Thomas More Society in Washington for a term during the '80s, they wanted my husband to give a talk on More. He graciously said he would. At that time he was not a Catholic but admired More from afar. When the day came, he gave a talk that many people said evoked the presence of More, as they listened to him. I can still remember the event. I had prayed to Saint Thomas as Bob was preparing the talk, and I think his experience of speaking to a Catholic group on that particular subject was instrumental in bringing my husband into the Church. I knew that anyone who could speak so well of this great man was not far from the Truth. When Bob was baptized a few years later, Thomas More was his patron saint.

As we face greater challenges to religious liberty, I think More's strong faith and amiable demeanor in the face of opposition will be an example I will try to hold on to, try to imitate, and especially share with young people who, in the digital age, think the past has nothing to teach them.

What difference does it make to know these stories, to know about these holy lives? They make all the difference. They remind us that we are part of a loving community rooted in Christ, and they are part of our lives. The saints of the Church, already in heaven, are able to intercede for us with Christ and through Christ. We can turn to them and ask their intercession for the grace we need. When we face difficult moments of decision making, loss of a job or a loved one, or are trying to right a wrong or to comfort the dying, we can turn to our holy friends, learn from their example, and feel the comfort of knowing we are not alone. We are in a community that beckons us

to greater growth in virtue and holiness through courageous example. We have an expanded horizon, unlike those without faith. As
followers of Christ, we can find friends across centuries and countries,
some of whom will remain with us for a lifetime.

A relationship with the saints requires some effort on our part.
Reading about their lives in books like the daily prayerbook *Magnifi-
cat* and reading biographies of the saints is a good beginning. We can
Google their lives, visit Catholic.org to read about the Saint of the
Day, follow the liturgical calendar, and become collectors of prayer
cards until we find our special patrons who inspire us to holiness.
Additionally, there are many devotions in honor of popular saints like
Saint Anthony of Padua, Thomas Aquinas, and, of course, Saint Patrick. Saint John Paul II canonized more saints than any other Pope
before him and gave us many new saints from the twentieth century,
including many laypeople; Pope Francis has canonized several hundred more saints than John Paul II. Both Popes knew we needed this
resource of holy people so we will never be discouraged from pur-
suing our own distinct call from Christ to follow Him and bring His
love to a lost and needy world.

Mary Ellen Bork

Joseph the Inadequate

"I will all the more gladly boast of my weaknesses, that the power of Christ may rest upon me.... [F]or when I am weak, then I am strong" (2 Cor 12:9–10). In this famous passage, Saint Paul gives expression to a fundamental principle of the Christian life. Now, the Apostle may have been the first to articulate it. But Saint Joseph was the first man to live it.

It may seem inappropriate, perhaps even impious, to talk about the "weaknesses" of Saint Joseph. There is, after all, a great need to praise his virtue and strengths. Especially in our culture, which demeans the nobility of being a husband, father, and worker, we need to grow in our estimation of this saint. He is so often hidden, passed over, or, worse, depicted as present but ineffectual—the old man shuffling along with Jesus and Mary.

And yet in our zeal to praise his virtue, we risk making Joseph not a just man but just a man. Strong, noble, pure, and kind—but still, just a man. It is reliance on grace, not natural goodness, that makes a man a Christian and a saint. And the experience of our weakness—as Saint Paul discovered—prompts us to that reliance.

Obviously, the kind of weakness here is not moral weakness, not sinful behavior or flawed character, not vice or foibles. Rather, it is weakness in the sense of insufficiency, of being inadequate, unequal to the task. Joseph's duty, after all, was not merely to do but to be—to be husband to the Virgin Mother and father to the Incarnate Word. No man, of course, is equal to that task. And throughout his mission, Joseph receives reminders of his inadequacy—as if Someone is trying to keep him dependent on grace.

Joseph first tries to acquit himself of the marriage because of his unworthiness to be Mary's spouse (see Mt 1:19).[3] Then in Bethlehem he cannot find decent lodging for his wife to give birth; he can only provide a stable for his wife and newborn Son (see Lk 2:7). At our Lord's circumcision (Lk 2:21) Joseph senses the superfluousness of his actions—providing covenantal ceremonies for the One Who

---

[3] See appendix 3 on p. 187 for further explanation on Joseph's unworthiness due to reverential fear of her holiness.

established the covenant. Likewise at the Presentation (Lk 2:22–38) he redeems the One Who not only needs no redemption but Who is Himself the Redeemer. On that same occasion Joseph hears prophecy of the sufferings to befall his wife and child—and rightly intuits his inability to protect them. Later he cannot defend his wife and child and so flees to Egypt (Mt 2:13–18). Upon his return, he finds that he cannot go back to his own town (Mt 2:19–23). And as if to add insult to injury, the last recorded event of Joseph's ministry to the Holy Family is his loss of the child Jesus in the Temple (Lk 2:41–52).

At every step, Joseph finds himself unequal to the task at hand. Now, a lesser man would react poorly to these experiences. He would respond perhaps peevishly—throwing up his hands in despondency or stamping his feet in frustration: "It's not fair!" Or he might ignore the signs of his limitations and vainly try to assert himself, raging against his weakness, trying to be strong—kicking "against the goads", as it was described to Saul of Tarsus (Acts 26:14).

Indeed, most of us, when face-to-face with our own inadequacy, either despair about it or rage against it. Our discouragement— "What's the point.... It's no use.... I give up"—depresses those around us and calls into question our confidence in God. Our futile assertiveness, on the other hand, frustrates us even more and makes us unbearable to those around us.

In Joseph we find the proper, the Christian, response. Scripture and Tradition both give the sense of Joseph's quiet, peaceful resignation—finding in his weakness an opportunity to lean more on God's strength. He does not buckle or rebel in the face of his own insufficiency. Rather, he turns such occasions into an opportunity to trust in God's power. By trusting in God's strength rather than his own, he taps into the proper source of true fatherhood.

This trust in the face of inadequacy shows Joseph to be truly the "Light of Patriarchs" and "Renowned Offspring of David", as the Litany of Saint Joseph names him. Saint Matthew establishes Joseph in the line of the patriarchs by tracing our Lord's genealogy from Abraham to Joseph (Mt 1:1–17). But Joseph shows himself a true son of Abraham, a true patriarch, not by mere bloodline but by his *trust*. Abraham confidently said, "God will provide," as he ascended Mount Moria to sacrifice his son (Gen 22:8). Joseph displays that same confidence in every instance of his weakness. And as David went out against Goliath, trusting not in his humble slingshot and stones but "in the name of the LORD of hosts, the God of the armies of Israel" (1 Sam 17:45), so Joseph, son of David, knows that the battle is the Lord's and He will be victorious.

Looking in the other direction of salvation history, Joseph sets the example for his Son's disciples. Indeed, in his trust that God will work through human weakness, he is the first man to follow his Son. Saint Peter learned this lesson later. By hard experience and bitter tears he saw that his strength was not enough to remain faithful, that God's grace alone could strengthen him to walk on water (Mt 14:22–36; Mk 6:45–56; Jn 6:16–21), to remain faithful, and ultimately to die a martyr (Mt 27:45–56; Mk 15:33–41; Lk 23:44–54; Jn 19:28–30). He first had to acknowledge his weakness and receive that grace. Likewise Saint Paul—a confident man, if ever there was one—learned through painful prayer that his weakness was no cause for despair but rather an occasion for trusting and encountering God's strength. Centuries later another Joseph would take comfort in the fact that "the Lord knows how to work and to act even with inadequate instruments."[4]

And we today learn the lesson again and again—that our weakness is no cause for discouragement, still less for rebellion. Our insufficiency occasions greater reliance on the Lord. Before all of us came Saint Joseph, as an example. He is that quiet, humble, hidden, and indeed inadequate man who trusted that the Lord's strength is made perfect in weakness, and who allowed his weakness to be transformed into strength.

John the Baptist: A Negative Witness

John the Baptist must have frustrated the priests and Levites sent out to learn who he was. Because he had nothing to say for himself. He only told them who he was not. "I am not," he says laconically

---

[4] "Urbi et Orbi Apostolic Blessing: First Greeting of His Holiness Benedict XVI", April 19, 2005, http://w2.vatican.va/content/benedict-xvi/en/speeches/2005/april/documents/hf _ben-xvi_spe_20050419_first-speech.html.

(Jn 1:20–21): not the messiah, not Elijah, not a prophet. He affirms only that he is a mere "voice of one crying out in the wilderness" (Jn 1:23; cf. Is 40:3; Mt 3:3; Mk 1:3; Lk 3:4). The Baptist's reaction may surprise us as well, living as we do in a culture that encourages us to talk, blog, and tweet about ourselves. It seems John is missing out on his fifteen minutes of fame. Surely, something is amiss.

On the contrary, nothing is wrong. The Baptist's modesty does not proceed from insecurity or uncertainty. He knows exactly who he is. But more importantly, he knows who he is not.

For their part, the crowds were not really sure who John was. They thought that he could be the messiah. Indeed, they were prepared to follow him as that. And John could have easily believed his own press. Most of us would have. It is evidence of his sanctity that he did not—that he preserved a sense of his own littleness, that he knew he was no more than a voice.

John's holiness and his proclamation of the Lord rest in great part on these words: "I am not." And the same is true with all subsequent holiness and evangelization, including yours and mine. The interior life and the spread of the Gospel begin with one's ability to make this simple negative statement: "I am not God." Without this negative there is no positive: the soul shrivels and the Gospel fails to spread. As regards the spiritual life, sin is in effect the refusal to say, "I am not God." Sin is to claim divine prerogatives, to claim that we are something we are not. Indeed, it is to take to ourselves the divine name and proclaim, "I am." Conversion and growth come about when we acknowledge ourselves as creatures and as sinners—as not God. Our Lord once said to Saint Catherine of Siena: "Do you know, daughter, who you are and who I am? If you know these two things you will have beatitude within your grasp. You are she who is not, and I am He Who is."[5] Granted, not the most flattering words from God to man, but they do provide a solid foundation for the spiritual life. They are in keeping with the first Beatitude: "Blessed are the poor in spirit" (Mt 5:3). Unless and until we recognize and confess that we are not God, then we cannot become what He wants to make us.

Further, as regards evangelization, we have to get out of the way. Anyone who wants to make Christ known must imitate the Baptist

[5] Raymond of Capua, *The Life of Catherine of Siena*, trans. Conleth Kearns (Dublin: Dominican Publications, 1980), 85.

and first confess that he is not the Messiah. The evangelist's task is not to announce himself but Someone else. Evangelical efforts stall and fail when we grow more concerned about who is doing the work than in the work being done, when we focus more on the one announcing than the One being announced. Unfortunately, the Church's history has many examples of men who preferred to announce themselves rather than the Lord—and as a result made a wreck of the Gospel.

"I am not," says the Baptist. And with those words he frees himself from the power of pride and opens the way for grace. "I am not," says the Baptist, and by so doing points the crowds to the One Who is. May we follow his example by acknowledging our nothingness—so that we can be filled with Christ's grace and point others to Him.

John the Baptist: A Messenger of Joy

In the Catholic Church's calendar, the Gospel readings about John the Baptist always fall during Advent, that time of preparation for Christmas. And he seems the most unlikely figure for that season. While we race around, anticipating Christmas, grabbing and consuming goods both durable and edible, John comes along with a message and a life of severity. He wore "a garment of camel's hair, and a leather belt around his waist; and his food was locusts and wild honey" (Mt 3:4). His greeting of Israel's leaders was similarly severe: "You brood of vipers! Who warned you to flee from the wrath to come?" (Mt 3:7). He probably was not the kind of guest you would invite to your Christmas party.

But Mother Church places him before her children precisely as we are preparing for Christmas—and for a good reason. Upon reflection we realize that John the Baptist is the perfect figure for Advent. He is the precursor of the Savior we await. Contrary to first impressions, he is the messenger of *joy*. His life and message remind us that Advent is not yet Christmas—that this penitential time leads to joy only if we heed its message. John the Baptist—who leaped for joy in his mother's womb (Lk 1:44)—is joy's perfect messenger because he shows us its necessary elements: repentance, humility, and sacrifice.

First, repentance. We confuse joy with pleasure. We think that joy is being content after a good meal; warm and well fed, lounging around in front of the TV, distracted, amused, entertained. But such things are fleeting and fragile. And even the beasts can enjoy them. Christian joy is something deeper and more lasting—indeed, eternal. It is spiritual, not physical, something that does not depend on things outside of us but in fact works from the inside out. It can coincide with physical and even deep emotional suffering. Most of all, it comes about not because we get our own way but because God's will is accomplished in us. In short, it comes from union with Him.

So the greatest obstacle to joy is *sin*, which separates us from the Lord. Thus John's message of repentance brings joy: it prompts us to leave sin behind and conform our wills to God's, to reestablish union with Him, our "exceeding joy" (Ps 43:4). Indeed, the mere knowledge of the possibility of being forgiven already causes rejoicing. The only sorrow greater than sin is not having a way out of it—being trapped in guilt and shame. John's call to repentance announces the One Who alone can free us. In short, our joy is *in a Savior*. And the only way to attain that joy is to acknowledge our sinfulness, our *need* to be saved.

Second, humility. John drew a lot of attention to himself. "Jerusalem and all Judea and all the region about the Jordan" went out to see him (Mt 3:5). They were ready to accept him as the Messiah. And yet he directed all the attention, honor, and reverence to our Lord. We, in our "Look at me!" culture, would delight in such attention. But John sends the crowds to Jesus. His parting words say it all: "He must increase, but I must decrease" (Jn 3:30).

If sin severs us from joy, pride blocks us from it. Pride insists on *my* way, that the world be on *my* terms. That attitude will never find joy, for it demands that it fit within our limited sphere of influence. By insisting that we are the ones who determine what is what, we contract our world and our capacity for joy. In fact, the proud do not really laugh or smile. They sneer at what does not fit in their world and smugly smirk at their supposed superiority.

By way of humility—by recognizing the truth of our relationship with God—we allow God to define things. And He does so much more broadly than we! Humility means to surrender our own space, not to be concerned about our ego, our own little world. Pride refuses the Lord entry out of fear of not having its own way.

Humility rejoices in God—and therefore in all circumstances. "He must increase, but I must decrease." The Lord's increase comes first. It gives motivation and meaning to our decrease. It enables us to rejoice in proportion to our diminishment.

Finally, *sacrifice*. John's asceticism—the simple clothes, the crude diet—is the first thing we notice about him. He did not live his life for this world. He was not out to make a name for himself, to become wealthy or popular—or even comfortable. His life was constantly being surrendered as a witness to Christ. This death-to-self that he practiced throughout his life realized its ultimate purpose in his martyrdom, his witness to the truth (see Mk 6:14–29).

To the world's eyes nothing could oppose joy more than mortification. The world tells us that joy is found doing your own thing, having whatever you want. And yet the sadness of our culture gives a clue about the error here. We live in the most prosperous culture in the history of the world. Even those of modest means enjoy luxuries that the emperors of the ancient world would envy. And yet our young people seem rudderless. We are discovering that the more we give the young what they want, the less capable and the less happy they seem to be.

John the Baptist shows that we attain joy only by the giving of ourselves—by renouncing ourselves and our own desires in the gift of self to another. This renunciation witnesses to the truth of higher, even eternal, goods. It puts false or fleeting "joys" in their place. No love and therefore no joy is possible without it.

The world brandishes before us many false joys. They are nothing more than passing pleasures, some coming with a hefty price tag. John the Baptist extends to us the truest joy—that of being in union with our Lord, experiencing His increase in our hearts, and serving Him generously.

John the Beloved and the Gifts of the Crucified

At the foot of the Cross stands only one of our Lord's Apostles. Of the Twelve, one betrayed him, one denied him, and all the others fled. Except John. He alone stands there, as a witness of our Lord's death and (doubtlessly) as a source of consolation to our Lord's Sacred Heart.

Saint John already enjoyed a privileged place among the Apostles. With Peter and James he received the great privilege of accompanying Jesus at three important events in His public life (the raising of the daughter of Jairus [Mk 5:37], the Transfiguration [Mt 17:1], and the Agony in the Garden [Mt 26:37]). But at Calvary John receives a far greater privilege than before. And he does so precisely because he perseveres with our Lord until the end.

First, our Lord gives John the gift of His own Mother. "When Jesus saw his mother, and the disciple whom he loved standing near, he said to his mother, 'Woman, behold, your son!' Then he said to the disciple, 'Behold, your mother!' And from that hour the disciple took her to his own home" (Jn 19:26–27). On a purely natural level, the dying Man desires that someone take care of and provide for His widowed Mother once He is gone. But there is a great deal more here. For He did not simply say, "Take care of my mother," or "Make sure she has what she needs." Rather, He gave Mary to John as His own mother. "Behold, your son.... Behold, your mother".

John's task therefore was principally of the heart: to love Mary as his own mother. This is made all the more clear by the fact that our Lord first commands *her* to take him as her son. That perfect affection and solicitude that Mary has for her Son, Jesus Himself directs to John. From that point she loves John as her own son. John receives, then, not only the grace to love Mary as his own mother, but also— and primarily—that Mary herself loves him as her own son.

As regards the second gift given to John, we get a glimpse of it at the Last Supper: John leans on the "breast of Jesus" (Jn 13:25). By so doing he comes into intimate contact with our Lord's Sacred Heart. Indeed, he leans right upon It. Our Lord granted to him alone that privileged intimacy. Now, as John stands beneath the Cross, that same Heart is pierced, and at once blood and water come out (Jn 19:34). He receives, then, the revelation—the opening— of our Lord's Sacred Heart. This is also the revelation of God the Father. "Just as Jesus, the Son, knows about the mystery of the Father from resting in his heart (cf. Jn 1:18), so too the Evangelist has gained his intimate knowledge from his inward repose in Jesus' heart."[6]

---

[6] Pope Benedict XVI, *Jesus of Nazareth: From the Baptism in the Jordan to the Transfiguration* (New York: Doubleday, 2007), 222.

Of course, our Lord intends these gifts not for John alone but for all His disciples—for us. John stands in our place at the Cross and receives these gifts on our behalf. It follows that to appreciate them we need to place ourselves at the foot of the Cross as well. It is there that Mary becomes our Mother and we her children. It is there that Christ's Sacred Heart is revealed (opened) and the love of the Father literally pours forth. If we desire a greater affection for our Lady and her maternal protection, we must receive her with John at the Cross. If we desire to enjoy that "inward repose in Jesus' heart", then we must be where that Heart is opened to all men. If we want to know the Father's love, we must go to where the Father is fully revealed. Only by persevering with John at the foot of the Cross can we also receive with John these divine gifts.

Mary Magdalene: The Power of Repentance

Although most of his friends abandoned Him, Jesus is not left completely alone at His Crucifixion. Of greatest consolation to him, of course, is His own Mother, accompanied by the Apostle John. But others are there as well, and tradition emphasizes one in particular: Mary Magdalene (Mt 27:55–56; Mk 15:40–41; Jn 19:25–26; cf. Lk 23:49). She is not just a footnote to the Crucifixion, however, but a powerful image of what every soul should bring to Calvary. In particular, she teaches us a truth we do not often consider: *the power of repentance.*

We typically think of repentance (if we think about it at all), as a negative. It is something difficult and distasteful that focuses on bad things—on the negatives. And yet repentance—that is, ongoing conversion—is essential to the Christian life. Without it we grow first complacent, then proud, and finally cold.

Now, we first encounter the Magdalene (as has been traditionally understood) at our Lord's feet in repentance: "[A] woman of the city, who was a sinner ... brought an alabaster flask of ointment, and standing behind him at his feet, weeping, she began to wet his feet with her tears, and wiped them with the hair of her head, and kissed his feet, and anointed them with the ointment" (Lk 7:37–38). So it is fitting (as Monsignor Ronald Knox observes[7]) that we find her again at our Lord's feet—at the foot of the Cross. Art typically depicts her standing with Mary and John, her long hair and her tears both flowing as a reminder of that initial repentance.

This time, however, her sorrow is different. Delivered from sin already, she no longer begs for forgiveness. Yet the years accompanying our Lord and growing closer to Him have produced both a deeper love for Him and a greater sorrow for sin. Indeed, her contrition has increased in direct proportion to her love.

Consider, then, the anguish of Mary Magdalene as she looks upon our Lord crucified. His death sets in relief what He means to her. She had perhaps grown accustomed to men treating her with disrespect, even using her. Christ had delivered her from that and had granted her the freedom from sin she thought she would never have. He now hangs crucified. Her deliverer is dead. In her heart well up both a renewed sorrow for sin and a deeper love for the One Who delivered her.

In short, Mary Magdalene's repentance brought her to a greater intimacy with the Lord. And this is the power of repentance. Had she not allowed sorrow to penetrate her heart, she would never have come to our Lord. Had she not heeded His call to repent (as we often do not), she would never have known Him. Had she hardened her heart (as we do), she would not have had the joy of knowing Him as the Savior. In a similar vein, Saint Augustine boldly calls her the "Archvirgin"[8]—because her repentance made her capable of giving herself wholly to Christ.

Not surprisingly, then, we also find in Mary Magdalene a model of contemplation. She was the one "who sat at the Lord's feet and listened to his teaching" and who sought the better part (Lk 10:38–42). She was at our Lord's feet again when He came to raise Lazarus (Jn 11:32). We find her now at the foot of the Cross, where she stands sorrowful—but contemplative. Or, rather, sorrowful *and*

[7] Ronald A Knox, *University and Anglican Sermons of Ronald A. Knox*, ed. Philip Caraman (London: Burns & Oates, 1962), 399.

[8] Saint Augustine, quoted in Fulton Sheen, *The Cross and the Beatitudes* (Tacoma, Wash.: Angelico Press, 2012), 32–33.

contemplative—because it is precisely her repentance that enables her contemplation. Her sorrow enables her to see our Lord better than those unwilling to weep for sin. Her tears do not cloud her sight but enhance it.[9]

The Magdalene obviously has particular importance for those who have led deeply sinful lives but have returned and have washed our Lord's feet with tears of repentance. Yet she also represents what every soul ought to bring to the Cross. Christ is the one who saves us from sin. Unless we acknowledge our need for a Savior—an acknowledgment that must be more than merely intellectual—we will not know the Savior. Repentance carries real power—the power to know Christ as Savior. And our deepening sorrow for sin in turn deepens our knowledge of the Savior.

Redeeming Peter

At the Transfiguration, Peter tells Jesus, "[I]t is well that we are here" (Mt 17:4; Mk 9:5). "Well, there he goes again," we think. Saint Peter always seems to interrupt and blurt out whatever comes to mind, and apparently with no sense of propriety. As the ancient writer Origen observed, Saint Peter "often appears in Scripture as hasty in putting forth his own ideas of what is right and expedient."[10] And so we find him at one moment asking to walk on water, then sinking for lack of faith (Mt 14:28–31). Then he is confessing our Lord as Son of the living God—and then blocking Him from His mission. At the Last Supper he pledges his life for the Lord (Mt 26:30–35), only to deny Him before sunrise (Jn 18:15–27; Lk 22:54–62; Mk 14:66–72). Yet we should also beware lest we dismiss Peter entirely. For we can learn a great deal from the Prince of the Apostles.

[9] The Church's history has had two different views of Mary Magdalene in the Gospels. The interpretation here follows the traditional understanding (embodied liturgically in the 1962 Missal) that Mary Magdalene was the same "sinful woman" of Luke 7, the Mary in Luke 10, and Mary of Bethany in John 13.

[10] Thomas Aquinas, *Catena Aurea: Commentary on the Four Gospels Collected out of the Works of the Fathers*, vol. IV, part II (Albany, N.Y.: Preserving Christian Publications, 2000), 425.

The Transfiguration provides a great case study. Overcome at the sight of our Lord glorified, Saint Peter exclaims, "Master, it is well that we are here; let us make three booths here, one for you and one for Moses and one for Elijah" (Mk 9:5; cf. Mt 17:4). Sure, it seems like another gaffe by Saint Peter, especially since He receives what amounts to a divine scolding: "This is my beloved Son; listen to him" (Mk 9:7; cf. Mt 17:5). But in fact he has the right instinct. He just jumps the gun a bit.

When Saint Peter beholds our Lord's glory, he sees it for what it is: the goal. Our Lord came into the world to win such glory—for Himself and for all men. By His Incarnation He took on our human nature. By His Passion and death He purified it. By His Resurrection and Ascension He glorified it. Heaven, the goal of human life, is to contemplate our Lord in glory and to be glorified with Him. Saint Peter immediately and instinctively senses (but perhaps does not yet understand) that the contemplation of Christ in glory is the greatest good. Naturally, he wants to stay: "Master, it is well that we are here; let us make three booths here, one for you and one for Moses and one for Elijah."

So instead of rolling our eyes at his mistake, let us appreciate Saint Peter's example. After all, most of us set the goal much lower than he. Few of us would even rise to the level of his mistake. How many of us truly see heaven—the vision of Christ face-to-face—as our life's goal? In truth, we would be content with far less: with material wealth, or comfort, a bit of fame perhaps, or power. At best people might possess the vague ambition to "make the world a better place". Eternal contemplation of Christ in glory somehow does not figure into most people's life goals. But Saint Peter knew it immediately.

Saint Peter goofed not in his words but in his timing. He wanted to contemplate Christ glorified—but before our Lord won that glory by His Passion and death. He wanted the prize without the contest. And again, this is a mistake we should be slow to criticize—we who would have the Gospel without sacrifice, holiness without prayer, virtue without effort, Communion without confession, and Easter without Lent. In a sense, Saint Peter reveals us to ourselves. In him we can see ourselves trying to find a shortcut, an easier route, a detour, some way of avoiding the Cross.

In the Catholic Church the account of the Transfiguration is always read on the second Sunday of Lent, while that penitential season is still young. By placing it there, Mother Church hopes to have us imitate Saint Peter's faith and avoid his hastiness. In Lent we accompany our Lord in the contest. We take upon ourselves some share of His suffering and death so that we will attain some share also of His eternal glory. May the clumsy but noble example of Saint Peter focus our thoughts on the ultimate goal and inspire us to accompany our Lord in the contest.

Fireside Chats

Peter drew near the charcoal fire. It was a cold night, and the fire offered him the warmth he desired. So he approached and warmed himself. By so doing he put himself in the company of his Lord's persecutors—who soon became his. They eventually recognized him as one of Jesus' followers and began to accuse him. He denied being in our Lord's company and soon denied our Lord himself. The cock crowed, and he wept bitterly (Mt 26:69–75; Mk 14:66–72; Lk 22:56–62; Jn 18:17–18, 25–27).

Unlike Judas, Saint Peter trusted that he could be forgiven. He persevered in his sadness and contrition until such a time that he could ask forgiveness and be restored to Christ. Our Lord's Resurrection brings forgiveness for Peter. And His appearance at the Sea of Tiberias is the occasion for Peter's rehabilitation (Jn 21:1–14). Once again Peter draws near a charcoal fire (Jn 21:9). This time, however, the fire promises not sin but redemption.

The very beginning of the scene already hints at something of a renewal for Saint Peter. Our Lord first called Peter while he was fishing and by way of a miraculous catch of fish (Mt 4:18–22; Mk 1:16–20; Lk 5:1–11; Jn 1:40–42). So also now, as if to signal a new beginning, our Lord comes to him. He appears on the shore and, unrecognized by the Apostles, commands them to cast their net off the right side of the boat. With that "they were not able to haul it in, for the quantity of fish" (Jn 21:6). The whole event reminds Peter of that moment years before when a similar miracle prompted him to leave everything and follow Jesus. With that, he leaps from the boat and rushes to our Lord (Jn 21:7).

When Peter reaches the shore he sees a charcoal fire, a reminder of a less noble moment in his discipleship. But as Peter's fall occurred before a fire, it is fitting that his redemption occur there as well. The rehabilitation undoes the fall. Peter approached the first fire seeking creature comfort (i.e., warmth). He approaches the second for supernatural reasons—to find Jesus. He came to the first at night, under cover of darkness. He comes to the second in the light of a new day. At that first fire he found himself among his enemies and, fearing shame, denied Jesus. At this second fire he finds himself with other disciples—and he is strengthened.

Within this context, then, our Lord invites Peter to atone for his denial. It is as though our Lord takes Peter back to the scene of the crime and gives him the opportunity to undo his sin. As our Lord's persecutors had asked Peter three times about his devotion to Christ, so now Jesus Himself does the same: "Simon, son of John, do you love me?" By his threefold affirmation of love—"Yes, Lord; you know that I love you" (Jn 21:15–17)—Peter undoes the knot that had kept him from the Lord. He then receives anew the invitation to discipleship: "Follow me" (Jn 21:19; cf. Lk 5:10, Mt 4:19).

At that second fireside chat, Jesus provides Peter an opportunity to participate in his own redemption. He has the chance to undo some of the harm he had done. What we see in Saint Peter's rehabilitation holds true for each one of us. God desires to associate us in His work of salvation. He alone redeems, but He desires that we participate. He alone forgives sin, but He wants to associate us in His work. He enabled Peter to do so by bringing him again to the fire and asking him again about his devotion. He enables us by way of confession, by acts of penance, by mortifications, by apologizing to those we offend, and by praying for those we have hurt. It is a glorious work that Jesus has accomplished in His death and Resurrection—more glorious still that He associates us with His work.

Veronica

Although she is not mentioned in Scripture, tradition tells us that Veronica was a woman who encountered our Lord as He carried the Cross and wiped His face with her veil. Afterward she found the miraculous imprint of His face on the cloth. The name Veronica comes from the Latin *vera icona*, meaning "true image". The name expresses her action and indicates what we can learn from her—or, rather, from Jesus through her.

First, there is the courage of this woman. It was a brutal scene—three convicted criminals being led to death, the weary and cynical soldiers, and of course the crowds following along to mock and scorn—much easier to remain apart from the whole situation. But she did not. And it could not have been an easy task to step forward to the condemned Man and wipe His face. What taunts or harassment must she have had to bear in order to reach Him? And having reached Him—what an awful sight. He was the "man of sorrows", as prophesied by Isaiah: "[M]any were astonished at him—his appearance was so marred, beyond human semblance.... He was despised and rejected by men; a man of sorrows, and acquainted with grief; and as one from whom men hide their faces" (Is 52:14; 53:3). Yet, she did not allow these difficulties to deter her from her mission. Charity, even of the simplest variety, requires courage.

Second, there is the power a simple act of charity carries. Although she surmounted considerable obstacles, her act of compassion was really quite simple. Indeed, given all that our Lord suffered, her gesture may seem negligible. All she did was wipe His face. And did she know Who He was? Did she know Him personally? Did she know about Him? Or was she just doing an act of kindness for someone she saw in need? Whatever the case, our Lord saw the depth of a seemingly insignificant gesture. Certainly she was to be rewarded: "I was in prison and you came to me" (Mt 25:36). Indeed, He rewarded her with an image of Himself.

We may hesitate at times to perform an act of charity or kindness because it may seem so small in the greater scheme of things. Veronica's action shows us the proper way to gauge the meaning and weight of our works—not by the action itself but by the devotion and love with which it is done.

Further, there is the image *received through an act of charity*. Tradition has it that in reward for her kindness, Jesus impressed on Veronica's veil the image of His Holy Face. So it was through Veronica's act of charity that our Lord's image was given to the world (as also the kindness of the women won for us the Shroud of Turin). So also, through our acts of charity the likeness of Christ continues—writ large, on the world stage. We make Him visible through simple but courageous acts of love.

Finally, our Lord chose to leave us an image of Himself *suffering*. There is no corresponding image of His birth or Baptism or even Resurrection—only of His Passion. The veil of Veronica (and the Shroud of Turin) seems to be of a piece with the Mass. At the Last Supper our Lord asked for only one thing to be done in His memory—the *sacrifice* of the Mass: "Do this in remembrance of me" (Lk 22:19; 1 Cor 11:24). We can see, then, an intersection here between charitable works and the sacrifice of the Mass: they both make our Lord present. The Mass, obviously, makes Him substantially present—Body, Blood, Soul, and Divinity. But our works of love proclaim His presence (make Him present) in another way.

VII

PRAYER

In Conversation with God

Introduction

by Helen M. Alvaré

Like so many people, I pray constantly throughout the day: for my husband and children, and extended family of course, and for friends and even acquaintances who share a particular need or sorrow with me. A traumatic car accident at age seventeen made such an impression upon me, that I pause to pray every time I hear a siren or see a tow truck with flashing lights. This can keep me pretty busy some days, as I live and work in two small cities. First thing in the morning as I'm rising, I petition God and several of my favorite saints to help direct my work that day, to do God's will and the good of others. At night I ask God to let my mind rest, and to remember that He is the Lord of all—and I am not.

It might all seem somewhat scattered. On deeper reflection, though, there is a unity to my eclectic prayer life. It is this: always, my prayers arise out of a prior effort to think of reality in God's larger and longer terms. I try to situate myself, and all those for whom I'm praying, in God's creation and God's realm, and then to petition, praise, and thank God, against a deeper reflection about what's true, what's important, what's real, as considered from that perspective.

There's a visual analogy for what I'm suggesting. My prayer context is like that special-effects technique in films when the camera either starts on a small, local object and pans back until it encompasses the Milky Way, or moves in the opposite direction. This is part of how I try to grasp "God's perspective" on the time-limited, local affairs about which I'm praying, and then to offer my praise, petition, and thanksgiving. Now that I'm getting old enough to actually get a glimpse of that "arc of history" everybody is always talking about, I am getting better at thinking broadly and about the long run.

An observer might conclude that, within this large perspective, I would bring very little to God in prayer. How could little things matter in such a big universe? But the observer would be wrong.

When I am praying about even one person (family or friend) the matter is instantly cosmic! There is a Spanish phrase that explains my thinking here: "cada persona es un mundo" (each person is a world). I feel perfectly assured that God cares a great deal about the health, happiness, self-worth, suffering, etc., of every single person. Humans are the pinnacle of creation. Pope Benedict XVI put it so gorgeously in *Deus Caritas Est* (God Is Love) when he instructed us to give every single person that "look of love which they crave".[1] Pope Francis, according to a first-person account related to me by a Roman friend, easily communicates the same view. At one of his weekly audiences in St. Peter's Square, the Pope heard a man shout to him, "You are one of a kind!" In the instant, the Pope stopped what he was doing to look back at the man and shout with equal warmth, "But you are one of a kind too!" No matter how long is history and how wide God's powers, I am confident that He still regards with favor my prayers holding up particular individuals.

It is also clear to me that the more I pray fervently for others, the more I learn to cosuffer with others, the more I am making the only kind of progress that counts in this life: learning to love. It teaches me also to affirm others' radical equality with me—and to understand my own suffering in context. It is some of my favorite prayer.

I also pray regularly for God to strengthen and direct my vocation—not because I am more important than anyone else, but because I know God gives each of us a vocation and wants us to live it out. As

---

[1] Pope Benedict XVI, Encyclical Letter *Deus Caritas Est*, December 25, 2005, no. 18, http://w2.vatican.va/content/benedict-xvi/en/encyclicals/documents/hf_ben-xvi_enc_20051225_deus-caritas-est.html.

a teacher, immersed in a world of verbiage (spoken and written), I ask God especially not to allow me to waste time and words on useless things. I ask Him to allow me to be the kind of teacher my students need. They are depending on me, and I need God's help.

I also beg Jesus (and "beg" is not too strong a word) to reach across two millennia, the changes in culture and language since biblical times, and to allow me to experience His Person, Whose genius, goodness, selflessness, supernatural command of the natural, and unsurpassed compassion for the other communicated clearly to onlookers and companions that this is the Messiah, Who alone can save us.

Finally, I have never let go of the "classics", foremost, the Our Father and the Hail Mary. No matter how much time has passed since their first articulation, they remain products of the mind and love of God. It's rare that I do not discover "something new", something currently pertinent, in one or more of their words or phrases on any given day.

Helen M. Alvaré

The Consoling Counselor

Like any important person, the Holy Spirit bears many titles. For example, our Lord calls Him "the Counselor" (Jn 14:16, 26; 15:26; 16:7). Another translation has "Advocate" (NIV); still others, "Consoler"[2] or "Comforter" (KJV). So which one is it? Counselor or Advocate? Consoler or Comforter? In one of those happy but rare occasions, they are all acceptable translations. In fact the ambiguity of the original Greek word helps reveal the Holy Spirit more. He is both Advocate and Comforter, Counselor and Consoler.

As Advocate or Counselor, He pleads our case before the Judge. The ancient Greek word means a legal attorney or counsel. (This may very well be the only text anywhere that describes God as a lawyer.) Yet unlike an advocate or counselor in this world, the Holy Spirit does not stand beside us to defend our case. Rather, He dwells within us, as the soul of our souls. From within us He appeals to God.

The Holy Spirit pleads our case in response to the devil, "the accuser" who night and day accuses us before God (Rev 12:10). The evil one tries to win our condemnation on the evidence of our sins. In response, the Holy Spirit stands as our Advocate. He wins our acquittal on the power of Christ's sacrifice, by which we have been redeemed and made children of God.

The Holy Spirit is likewise our Advocate in the world. He instructs us in the truth so that we can faithfully witness to Christ. He commands us what to say and, just as importantly, what not to. And again, He does this not from the outside as One apart from us, but interiorly as One united to our very souls. Our Lord describes Christian witness in just this way: "[I]t is not you who speak, but the Spirit of your Father speaking through you" (Mt 10:20).

Most of all, the Holy Spirit is our Advocate in prayer. He prays from within us, bringing our prayers to our heavenly Father in His own voice. "It is the Spirit himself bearing witness with our spirit that we are children of God" (Rom 8:16). He "helps us in our weakness; for we do not know how to pray as we ought, but the Spirit himself

[2] See *The Catholic Study Bible*, ed. Donald Senior (New York: Oxford University Press, 1990), 172.

intercedes for us with sighs too deep for words" (Rom 8:26). He is our Advocate in the most intimate and personal sense.

Yet the Greek word here can also mean "Comforter" or "Consoler". In striving to live as faithful Catholics, we inevitably suffer setbacks and persecution. This side of heaven, in this vale of tears, we should expect difficulties. So where will we find the comfort we need? How will we be consoled? Will we seek true or false comfort? The enduring comfort of heaven, or the passing comfort of the world? All around us we see people seeking comfort in food, sex, drugs, mindless entertainment, etc. Such comfort passes quickly and leaves a person worse off than before.

The Holy Spirit (Advocate, Comforter, and Consoler) is also "the Spirit of truth" (Jn 16:13). His comfort is greater than anything in this world because it is rooted in the truth. He does not bring a false mercy or consolation. He brings the truth that itself consoles. Our Lord connects this consolation with being God's children. His words "I will not leave you desolate" (Jn 14:18) can also be translated "I will not leave you as orphans"(NIV). In the midst of the world's trials, the greatest comfort we have is that we are God's children.

So the Holy Spirit works in two directions. As Advocate He works from down here, appealing for us upward to God. As Comforter, He works from up there, bringing God's consoling truth down to us. He brings our prayers and defense before God's throne. And He brings God's grace, peace, and love to us here below.

A Place in the Country

We hear several times in the Gospels that our Lord removes Himself from the crowds and goes off by Himself. As Mark explains, this was due partly to His miracles: due to His fame, "Jesus could no longer openly enter a town, but was out in the country; and people came to him from every quarter" (Mk 1:45). But fame and first-century paparazzi were not the only reasons for such seclusion. It was a common practice for Him. He would rise "a great while before day" and go to a deserted place and pray (Mk 1:35; cf. Mt 13:1; Lk 4:42; 5:16).

Further, He taught His Apostles to do the same: "Come away by yourselves to a lonely place, and rest a while" (Mk 6:31). Hermits, monks, and nuns have imitated this removal from society throughout the Church's history. And yet it seems a strange thing: the crowds come to Jesus for healing—and He goes off on His own? And as for us, there is a lot of work to be done. Can we really afford the luxury of getting away from it all and finding a little place in the country?

In fact, we cannot afford not to take such time as our Lord did. He was not, of course, just "getting away from it all", as we might fashion such retreats to the country. Rather, He was going to the One Who is All—to His Father. He removed Himself from the crowds not because He had enough of them (He is not like us in that regard), but to give Himself "in prayer to God" (Lk 6:12). He retreated so that He could enter into uninterrupted conversation with His Father.

Yet the crowds would follow Him (Mk 6:33–34). Perhaps they sensed (without realizing) that it was precisely our Lord's union with His Father, so dominant during His retreats, that drew them to Him. He brought them not just miracles nor only a message of salvation. He brought them His own personal knowledge of the Father. He brought them the very intimacy of that union.

Hermits and monks of the Church have experienced this same phenomenon. When they remove themselves from society to give themselves more completely to God, crowds follow. When Saint Anthony of Egypt went into the desert to seek holiness, he soon had people seeking him out. When Saint Benedict turned aside from Rome to seek conversion of life, he soon had a monastery. In both instances (and in hundreds like them in the Church's history), one man's desire for union with God led to great works for the Gospel.

The world views such seclusion as a waste of time and even self-ish. Of course, unless a thing can be measured (preferably counted and deposited), the world has no use for it. No matter: the Gospel works by different standards. The first step in the work of the Gospel is union with God. Evangelization begins by first going to God and deepening our union with Him—without that, there is nothing. The crowds today, no less than any other time, desire not just a message nor even miracles. They desire—indeed, need—persons who know God. They need saints.

Not many of us have a place in the country to go and spend time in prayer. But we are all called to imitate our Lord by seeking first that intimacy with the Father. So we should carve out time and a suitable place to remove ourselves from the crowds and pray to our "Father who is in secret" (Mt 6:6). It is that conversation, that nourishment of our union with Him, that enables us to bear witness more effectively. Yes, we should study our faith and do good works. But by placing prayer first, we guarantee that when we return to the crowds, they will encounter in each of us not just someone who knows the truth and does good, but, of greatest importance, someone in union with God.

Hide and Seek

Only those who love can understand the game of "hide and seek". Parents and children play this game, as did lovers in more innocent days. They understand how a loved one's temporary absence increases the desire to see him, and how the heightened anticipation of finding him increases the joy when at last he is found. They play the game not to frustrate or anger each other but to cultivate a greater joy in seeing one another.

This simple game helps explain why our risen Lord hides Himself from His disciples at certain times and shows Himself at others. At the Sea of Tiberias, for example, He stood on the shore and called out. "[Y]et the disciples did not know that it was Jesus" (Jn 21:4). They eventually recognized the Lord only because He "revealed Himself" (Jn 21:1). A similar thing happened when Mary Magdalene encountered Him at the tomb: before He made Himself known, she thought it was "the gardener" (Jn 20:15). So also the disciples on the road to Emmaus: until the breaking of the bread, "their eyes were kept from recognizing him" (Lk 24:16). And even then He immediately "vanished out of their sight" (Lk 24:31).

I hope it is not irreverent to characterize our Lord's mysterious concealing and revealing of Himself as a divine form of hide and seek. He hides Himself not to frustrate or to avoid His disciples, but to entice them to search for Him. He conceals Himself to cultivate in their hearts the desire to see Him and the resolve to look for Him. He hides so that in loving Him they will seek Him and that in seeking Him they will love Him more.

This game of hide and seek is nothing new. We find it throughout Scripture. The psalmist cries out, "When shall I come and behold the face of God?" (Ps 42:2), and asks the Lord, "How long will you hide your face from me?" (Ps 13:1). Such passages confirm our own experience: sometimes it seems as though the Lord hides from us. Our prayer grows cold and routine, our petitions go (seemingly) unanswered, and our spiritual growth appears stunted. He is nowhere to be found. At those times we face the temptation to give up and stop looking. Abraham, King David, and Job faced similar temptations, as did just about every saint in heaven.

At those moments, however, we should redouble our efforts. Precisely then, when we have no sense of our Lord's presence, we proceed by faith more than anything else. And that increases our faith. This goes a long way to answer the age-old question of why God hides Himself: He hides so that we will search, and in searching we will grow in faith.

He entices us to search for Him also so that our love will grow. Love first inspires the search, because love always seeks the beloved. At the Sea of Tiberias, therefore, Saint John, "[t]hat disciple whom Jesus loved" (Jn 21:7)—that is, the Apostle most representative of love—recognized Him before anyone else. Then, having initiated the search, love itself increases as we desire to find Him. "The entire life of a good Christian is in fact an exercise of holy desire," says Saint Augustine.[3] "You do not yet see what you long for, but the very act of desiring prepares you, so that when He comes you may see and be utterly satisfied."[4] If the Lord seems distant or hidden, it is so that our love will prompt the search and the search will increase our love.

The obscurity or hiddenness of the Lord should not discourage us. Rather, it should inflame our desire to see Him all the more. This is

---

[3] Augustine's Tractate 4 on the Epistle of John, Section 6 (*Liturgy of the Hours*, vol. 3 [New York: Catholic Book Publishing, 1975], p. 220).
[4] Ibid.

the way of faith and love. The greatest sadness comes not from the difficulty in finding the Lord, but from the refusal to seek Him at all.

Learned Ignorance

"Lord, teach us to pray" (Lk 11:1). This plea from our Lord's disciples expresses the desire of every human heart. Man was created for intimacy with God. And for a time he enjoyed such a union, in his original state of justice. The fall of Adam disrupted that intimacy, and ever since we have been trying to get back to that initial gift of conversation with God. Jesus came to restore that intimacy and to answer the frustrated desire of the human heart for genuine prayer. The Church continues our Lord's work of teaching His disciples what and how to pray. Her reflection on our Lord's life and her fidelity to his words has produced in the Church a great wisdom about prayer. Many people go chasing after new and exotic methods of prayer. As a result, they miss the treasury of wisdom about prayer that the Church carries within herself.

The first step of prayer is to realize that we do not know how to pray. Our Lord teaches us just that through the words of the Apostle Paul: "[W]e do not know how to pray as we ought" (Rom 8:26). He likewise teaches us Himself, "[Y]our Father knows what you need before you ask him" (Mt 6:8). These words indicate not that there is no point in asking our Father, but that He knows better than we what we need.

We do not really know what we need. We begin to pray the moment we say in all honesty and humility, "Lord, I do not know how to pray." One spiritual writer uses the phrase *pons asinorum* (the bridge of the asses) to describe this phenomenon.[5] The recognition that we are ignorant (like asses) is the bridge that brings us into prayer.

Far from being a reason for discouragement, ignorance about prayer is the starting point. "Blessed are the poor in spirit" (Mt 5:3); that is, blessed are they who know that spiritually they do not have

---

[5] Eugene Boylan, *The Priest's Way to God* (Westminster, Md.: Newman Press, 1962), 65.

what they need and must rely entirely on God. Such awareness of ignorance and poverty opens our souls to the work of the Holy Spirit: the Spirit who "helps us in our weakness", the Spirit who "himself intercedes for us with sighs too deep for words" (Rom 8:26). If we are full of ourselves, of our own strength and ability—if we have delusions of sufficiency—then the Holy Spirit will find no room to work and pray from within us. Once we acknowledge our weakness and ask for help in prayer, *then* the Holy Spirit can begin His work of praying from within us and forming the habit of prayer within us.

"We do not know how to pray as we ought." This explains why so many of us avoid prayer. We make up many excuses for why we do not pray: "I'm too busy.... God already knows what I need.... My life is a prayer." But in reality, the reason we do not pray is because it brings us face-to-face with our limitations, with our insufficiency, with the fact that He is God and we are not. Nonbelievers depict prayer as a refuge for the weak and ignorant. In reality, there is nothing more adventurous, risky, and intimidating than prayer. It brings us to our knees.

But for all that, prayer should not frighten us. If you have ever felt helpless in prayer, take heart. Make the disciples' cry of the heart your own: "Lord, teach us to pray." Once we have done that, we have already begun to pray—we have begun the adventure and romance that will define the rest of our lives.

Preparation: What Are You Doing Here?

God found Elijah hiding in a cave on a remote mountainside. The prophet was a long way from home (a forty-day journey, to be exact). So the Lord asked him, "What are you doing here, Elijah?" (1 Kings 19:9). It was a good question. What *was* he doing there? The divine question forced Elijah to consider all the recent events of his life—his confrontation with the priests of Baal, his flight from persecution, the miraculous food provided for him, his forty-day journey to Mount Sinai. Only after some thought and reflection could he gather all these together and begin to speak with the Lord. Only then could he begin to pray.

Most likely, when we set ourselves to pray we will not find ourselves in as dramatic a setting as Elijah. Certainly we can and must pray to the Lord often by means of what the Church Fathers called "javelins", short, targeted prayers that we throw up to heaven. But the *deeper* conversations with God begin the same way as Elijah's did, with a consideration of why we are praying. In a certain sense, when we begin prayer God asks us, "What are you doing here?" We should not imagine that His tone is one of impatience or annoyance ("What are *you* doing here?"). Rather, we should hear Him ask in a tone of genuine concern and interest. After all, He already knows what we need. He does not need to think about what we are doing in prayer; we need to. So He asks us, "What are you doing here?" to prompt us to reflect on why we are praying in the first place.

Which is all to say that prayer demands *preparation*. Spiritual writers speak of *remote* and *immediate* preparation. Taken broadly, remote preparation indicates simply keeping a lifestyle compatible with and conducive to prayer. If we habitually fall into mortal sin, remain steeped in vice, and have no intention to reform ourselves, then we should not be surprised that we encounter difficulty in prayer. We need to repent first. More specifically, remote preparation is to identify *ahead of time* the when and how of prayer. What time will we make for prayer, and how will we spend it? What prayers will we say? What will we meditate on? What will we tell God? As with any important human endeavor, prayer demands planning ahead.

Immediate preparation is how we settle ourselves in order to pray. Most of us have the experience of not being able to focus our minds in prayer. They keep wandering to anything *except* prayer: work around the house, issues at the office, groceries ("and I wonder if those things are still on sale"), family, friends, and so forth. We need some time to settle down into prayer and get the wandering to stop. One wise priest calls this "dieseling". Remember how a diesel engine would sputter and run on before it rested? So also we need a certain period of time at the beginning of prayer to "diesel", to settle down and focus our hearts and minds.

One help to get us to settle is a prayer to begin prayer—that is, to ask for the ability to focus our thoughts and affections. Then, once we have settled and focused (as best we can in this world), we can begin to answer that question of God: "What are you doing here?"

The Prayer of Adoration

The highest and most important form of prayer is adoration. Unlike the other forms of prayer (petition, reparation, thanksgiving), adoration rests not so much on a consideration of what God has done or can do for us. Rather, it responds simply to the fact that He *is*. And for that reason it may be the most difficult form of prayer to understand. It seems to be the least concrete form of prayer. Petition expresses our needs, reparation our sorrow, and thanksgiving our gratitude—all for concrete, specific things. But adoration, while including these, also moves beyond them to God Himself, simply because He is.

The *Catechism of the Catholic Church* states:

> Adoration is the first act of the virtue of religion. To adore God is to acknowledge him as God, as the Creator and Savior, the Lord and Master of everything that exists, as infinite and merciful Love.... To adore God is to acknowledge, in respect and absolute submission, the "nothingness of the creature" who would not exist but for God. (*CCC* 2096–7)

All of this may seem somewhat disconnected from what we call "real life" and the "real world". Indeed, those who offer time in adoration may suffer criticism for *wasting* time or fleeing. But the opposite is true: by adoration we do not flee the real world or real life. Rather, by adoration we interact with the greatest reality, and the only necessary reality. Adoration brings us into contact with Life itself. The so-called "real world" and "real life" are in fact passing, temporal things. At some point they will not be. What "real life" presented to us yesterday as important means nothing today. What the "real world" demands of us today it will forbid tomorrow. God alone is eternal, lasting, and necessary. Time spent in adoration of

Him is time spent with the ultimate reality, with "the life which is life indeed" (1 Tim 6:19).

The *Catechism* brings out another implication for day-to-day living: "The worship of the one God sets man free from turning in on himself, from the slavery of sin and the idolatry of the world" (*CCC* 2097). We face a stark choice: we worship and adore *either* God *or* created things. We are created for the purpose of worship and adoration. We *will* adore something or someone. The question is, will we adore God or a creature? When we worship created things—money, pleasure, prestige, fame, etc.—we become slaves to them. We reduce our lives to a very pinched, narrow existence. When we worship God, however, we enter into the infinite plenitude of His world and life.

Finally, time spent in adoration expresses and perfects our love. Adoration comes from love; we adore what we love. When a man loves a woman, he may very well say that he adores her and only has eyes for her. A mother will look at her infant child in loving adoration. This love looks only to the person, not to any benefit received or potential gain. As the philosopher Joseph Pieper observes, to love someone is to say, "It is good that you exist."[6] And that is what we do in adoration—to have eyes only for God and to rejoice that He exists.

The Power of Thanksgiving

It is one of the first things that parents teach their children: to give thanks. They encourage them to say, "Thank you", and to make sure they write illegible little thank-you cards after Christmas or a birthday. We seem never to forget this childhood lesson. Our words and cards become perhaps more perfunctory, but they still salute the basic duty to give thanks. And even when we fail to give thanks (perhaps more often than not), we still acknowledge its importance.

In relation to God, thanksgiving is even more fundamental, the first duty of the creature to the Creator. Saint Thomas Aquinas locates

---

[6] Joseph Pieper, *Faith, Hope, Love* (San Francisco: Ignatius Press, 1977), 174.

the prayer of thanksgiving within his treatise on justice. We have an *obligation* to give thanks. The Mass also calls this to mind. "Let us give thanks to the Lord our God," says the priest. "It is right and just," the people respond. It's not just a good idea or a nice thing every now and then, but a matter of justice and of conduct worthy of God.

Perhaps because it is such a basic duty, we lose sight not only of the importance but also of the *power* of thanksgiving. Repeated acts of thanksgiving give the mind the proper perspective on things. They shape the soul, perfecting it more and more in a right relationship with God. We run the risk of reducing thanksgiving to just good etiquette and manners, to duty and justice. In reality, giving thanks to God, not just once a year, but repeatedly and often, perfects us as His children. It maintains the proper relationship with Him. He is God and we are not. By voicing our indebtedness, we learn more and more just how poor in spirit we are, that without Him we "can do nothing" (Jn 15:5).

Thanksgiving brings into perspective also the world's problems and our failures. We know very well when things go wrong and, if we have any self-knowledge whatsoever, when we do wrong. But problems in the world and in us are not the most important or even the first things to see. God's goodness comes before any of these. Thus Saint Ignatius teaches that the first step in the examination of conscience (what he calls the "general examen") is to think not of our sins but of God's goodness—that is, to give thanks.[7] The most fundamental truth about our relationship with God is not our rebellion against Him but His goodness to us. To think of our sins without first considering His gifts puts our sinfulness ahead of His goodness. And no one who thinks that way will trust in His mercy. Before "I'm sorry" comes "Thank you."

So also thanksgiving generates confidence for the future. In her prayer, ancient Israel always recounted first what the Lord had done in the past (creation, the Exodus, the Covenant, the Kingdom) and only then asked for His gifts (blessing, forgiveness, protection, deliverance). The more we reflect on what He has done for us in the past, the more confidence we will have for the future. This is the shape of

---

[7] Saint Ignatius, *The Spiritual Exercises of Saint Ignatius of Loyola* (New York: Catholic Book Publishing, 1948), 43.

the Mass, of the Eucharistic (i.e., thanksgiving) sacrifice: the great-est act of His goodness is made present as we make petition for the future.

Although in prayer we typically race ahead and ask God for what we need, the prayer of thanksgiving really should precede that of peti-tion. Jesus tells us, "[W]hatever you ask in prayer, believe that you receive it, and you will" (Mk 11:24). We will not believe in that manner unless we first recall His goodness and deliberately thank Him for what He has *already* done. In addressing the European Parliament in 2014, Pope Francis spoke about "protecting memory and hope".[8] The two things are essential to each other, because without memory there can be no hope. This is the Judeo-Christian tradition of prayer: we remember with thanksgiving the good He has done in the past so as to hope more confidently that He will do good in the future.

To illustrate this connection between thanksgiving and petition, Saint Thomas Aquinas points to a prayer from the Mass: "Through giving thanks for benefits received we merit to receive yet greater benefits" (post-Communion prayer from the common of a confessor bishop).[9] By giving thanks we widen our hearts in trust of God and so therefore increase our capacity to receive what He desires to give us. Brilliantly abbreviating this whole point, simple Father Solanus Casey says, "Thank God ahead of time."[10]

Finally, thanksgiving should be specific. It is not a vague attitude, a nod of the head to God's goodness as a theological truth. Our thanks should be for specific things, for life, health, rain, snow, a leaf, a kind word, a smile, and most of all for the Host placed upon the tongue. We should give thanks also for our crosses, for those difficulties that provide an opportunity for us to walk with Him, to accompany Him in the act of redemption.

It is one of the first things that parents teach their children—and that the Father teaches us. The more we thank Him, the more we

[8] "Address of Pope Francis to the European Parliament", November 25, 2014, http://w2 .vatican.va/content/francesco/en/speeches/2014/november/documents/papa-francesco _20141125_strasburgo-parlamento-europeo.html.

[9] Thomas Aquinas, *Summa theologica* II–II, q. 83, art. 17.

[10] Solanus Casey, O.F.M.Cap. quoted in Michael H. Crosby, O.F.M.Cap., *Thank God Ahead of Time: The Life and Spirituality of Solanus Casey* (Cincinatti, Ohio: St. Anthony Mes-senger Press, 2009), 145.

know Him as a loving Father and ourselves as His children, confident in His goodness—past, present, and future.

The Prayer of Reparation

If we dedicate ourselves to the prayer of petition, it will not be long before we realize that we deserve nothing of what we ask. Thus we progress logically into the prayer of reparation or repentance. In the prayer of thanksgiving we acknowledge that we are creatures dependent on the Creator's goodness. In the prayer of reparation we recognize that we are sinners in need of His mercy.

Prayer must always be rooted in truth. And, contrary to trendy thinking, the truth is that we labor under the burden of a human nature wounded by sin. Moreover, we ourselves have at times chosen against God and the order of His creation. We have offended the very One to Whom we pray. Thus we do not pray simply to feel good or get in touch with a cosmic force. We pray because we need to be healed of sin and strengthened against temptation. Neglect of this truth leads to presumption in prayer. When we pray we do not negotiate with God from a position of strength. Rather, we come to Him as we are: sinful creatures. Only then can we recognize Who He is: the merciful provider.

Repentance should always characterize our prayer. It sets the tone for the conversation. Every conversation begins with some statement (no matter how casual) about the speakers. So prayer ought to begin with a brief summary of who we are and Who He is. The Mass trains us in this. The first movement of Mass is always to acknowledge our sinfulness and God's mercy. Either in the Confiteor ("I confess to Almighty God ...) or the Asperges (the Sprinkling Rite), we begin our prayer with a statement of the interested parties: we, sinners in need of redemption, and He, the merciful and redeeming God.

Unless we acknowledge this from the beginning, the rest of our prayer will be off course because it will lack the truth about ourselves and about Him.

So the prayer of repentance concerns, first of all, our own sins. We come before God to ask mercy and forgiveness for what we have done and failed to do. Such repentance may be for sins that we need to confess in the Sacrament of Penance. Or it may be to ask for healing of the lingering wounds of sins already confessed. Whatever the case, prayers of reparation establish a more candid and open dialogue with God. By laying bare our wounds, we open more of ourselves to His grace.

The modern mind-set sees such repentance as demeaning or somehow not in accord with our dignity. The fact is, to repent means to recognize ourselves as morally responsible creatures. No small dignity, that! Nor does repentance lessen the power of our prayer. Rather, repentance enhances our prayer because our greatest claim on His mercy is our sinfulness.

Reparation also means praying for God's mercy toward others. Sin abounds in this world, and those who pray must ask God's mercy not only for themselves but also for the whole world. Thus Abraham prayed for Sodom and Gomorrah, and Moses prayed (more successfully) for the Israelites (Gen 18:22–23; Ex 32:11–14, 31–34). We who live in the culture of death should offer prayers of reparation for the sins of our society. Indeed, we Christians (other Christs) have an obligation to the world to offer such prayers, to imitate Him Who offered prayers of reparation as He hung upon the Cross.

The Prayer of Petition

To pray means, in its most basic sense and in every language, to *ask* for something. Thus perhaps the most fundamental kind of prayer is that of petition, the bringing of our needs before God. We know this truth instinctively when we find ourselves in need, when financial, family, or health problems besiege us. And we do well to ask His help at such times. Of course, it would not be right to pray *only* when we are in need (but by the same token, it would be foolish not to pray at such times). We must pray at other times as well—and *ask* for things in prayer at other times, whether or not we feel the need. We must recognize that we are always in need of God's assistance—and pray accordingly.

The point is, we ought to ask for things in prayer. To do so is not selfish or self-serving. Certainly an individual can go about such petition with the wrong motive or attitude. But that blame falls to the individual, not the prayer. God actually desires that we ask for what we need. Indeed, He commands it. "Ask, and it will be given you; seek, and you will find; knock, and it will be opened to you" (Mt 7:7). He reserves His words of rebuke not for those who ask for help but for those who do not ask—because they think they do not need Him.

We should root our prayer of petition in two complementary truths: human weakness and divine goodness. First, we ask for help precisely because we need it—because we are creatures in need of a Creator and sinners in need of a Redeemer. We do not ask for divine assistance because we deserve it. For no one can make a claim on God's assistance and mercy. Our weakness and need is our greatest claim on His generosity and mercy.

Second, our prayer of petition rests on God's goodness. We should not imagine God as a stingy, grumpy deity who is otherwise occupied and has no time for our concerns. Rather, He is the Father Who provides for His children more faithfully, more generously, and more wisely than any earthly father. "If you then, who are evil, know how to give good gifts to your children, how much more will your Father who is in heaven give good things to those who ask him!" (Mt 7:11).

Of course, God also desires that we ask with the proper attitude and disposition—namely, faith. The more profoundly we trust, the more our prayers will be answered. This is another truth we come across often in the Gospels. Men and women receive healing (i.e., the answer to prayers) because they had faith, they trusted. So trusting faith must be the leading edge in our prayer. "Therefore I tell you, whatever you ask in prayer, believe that you receive it, and you will" (Mk 11:24).

Nevertheless, we should not think of God as a divine vending machine, obliged to spit out exactly what we request. No, when we ask for something in faith, we ought also to look beyond what we think we need and abandon ourselves to what God knows we need. When we enter into the prayer of petition, we ask for some good. While we focus on the temporal or lesser good in mind, God may very well skip ahead and give us some greater good we had not considered. Thus our Lord says in another place, "If you then, who are evil, know how to give good gifts to your children, how much more will the heavenly Father give *the Holy Spirit* to those who ask him!" (Lk 11:13; italics added). More than anything else we can imagine or request, God desires to give us the Holy Spirit—grace, holiness, salvation.

VIII

THE LIFE OF GRACE

Christic within Us

Introduction

by Daniel Mattson

The older I get, the more keenly I become aware of how weak a man I am. The signs come to me daily: a faceless motorcyclist zooms into my rearview mirror, impatient that I'm in his way. As he zips by me, treating me and my car as part of his personal slalom course, I'm tempted to fly him the bird. And sometimes I do.

As I walk down a street in the heat of summer and see more skin than modesty should allow, my eyes easily dart hither and yon, contemplating what I would like to do with the bodies I see. Too often I just see objects to be used. They become flesh, not souls. Not persons.

Someone at work dishes up a juicy secret around the water cooler. It titillates me, and I have a story to share in return. I eat that second cookie I swore I wouldn't eat. Then I have a third, followed by "just a half". Five minutes later, I make it an even four.

Time and time again I fall short of the sort of noble life I would like to lead. I'm reminded daily of the words of Saint Paul: "I can will what is right, but I cannot do it. For I do not do the good I want, but the evil I do not want is what I do" (Rom 7:18–19).

In falling short and in seeing my weakness, I know that I am made for better stuff than I settle for. When I lack discipline, or am quick to anger, it's not a puritanical guilt that makes me regret my actions.

No, it's the inherent sense within me that I am made to be better than I am.

We're a society obsessed with becoming "better than we are". We seem to always know we are in need of self-improvement. The self-help section of any bookstore reveals how much man realizes he can—and should—be better than he is. But why do we strive so much for self-improvement, unless we know innately that we are the sort of creatures who desperately need help to become better "selves"?

Saint Paul seems to be speaking for every man who has faced the darkness and weakness of his own heart when he cries out, saying, "Wretched man that I am! Who will deliver me from this body of death?" (Rom 7:24). And yet—all is not lost. Saint Paul answers triumphantly, "Thanks be to God through Jesus Christ our Lord!" (Rom 7:25). Christ came that we might "have life, and have it abundantly" (Jn 10:10). But what does the abundant life look like? How do we live our lives, "and have it abundantly"?

We only begin to truly live when we enter into the life of grace, which is the life of Christ within us.

When we are weak, or desire to be better than we are, we know the words of Saint Paul are true: "[A]ll have sinned and fall short of the glory of God" (Rom 3:23). Those words aren't about the wrath of God, as I once thought when I was a child. Rather, I see them now as a lament, filled with sorrow for man's state. But the good news of the Gospel is that though we all fall short, we "are justified by his grace as a gift" (Rom 3:24). It is the gift of God's grace that allows us to reclaim the fallen glory of God. It is an invitation to life, to fully live as we were created to be, for, as Saint Irenaeus taught us, "the glory of God is man fully alive".[1] This is only accomplished through the work of Christ in us, supporting our weakness with his strength.

As the German philosopher Josef Pieper observed, it is our participation in the life of grace, the virtue that only Christ brings us, that allows us to realize in our lives "an ennobling of man's nature that entirely surpasses what he 'can be' of himself". He writes, "This supernatural potentiality for being is grounded in real, grace-filled participation in the divine nature, which comes to man through Christ (2 Pet 1:4)."[2]

---

[1] Saint Irenaeus, *Adv. haeres* 4, 20, 7: PG 7/1, 1037; quoted in *CCC* 294.
[2] Joseph Pieper, *Faith, Hope, Love* (San Francisco: Ignatius Press, 1997), 99.

In Baptism we put on Christ, becoming in actuality Him. The life of grace is Christ in me, conquering the weaknesses within me that I cannot overcome through my own efforts.

The life of grace isn't Christ walking beside me, or even carrying me like the popular poem "Footprints in the Sand" would suggest. There's only ever one set of footprints: Christ in me and me in Christ. As Saint Paul tells, "[I]t is no longer I who live, but Christ who lives in me" (Gal 2:20).

We are forever invited to put on Christ. Though we fall short, our heavenly Father is always quick to welcome us home, looking for us from afar, ready to bind our wounds, forgive our sins, slay the fatted calf, and clothe us ever anew in His Son (cf. Lk 15:11–32). "[W]here sin increased, grace abounded all the more" (Rom 5:20) becomes our hope in the face of our own weakness. And in each moment of reconciliation, we are invited to go ever deeper into the life of grace, of allowing the divine life of Christ to permeate our lives.

Our weakness is actually a gift, for it is the key that unlocks the door that invites us to participate in the life of Christ. As Christ said to Saint Paul, "My grace is sufficient for you, for my power is made perfect in weakness" (2 Cor 12:9). Saint Paul's example shows us the path that opens up the life of grace to us. In our weakness, let us say along with him, "I will all the more gladly boast of my weakness, that the power of Christ may rest upon me.... [F]or when I am weak, then I am strong" (2 Cor 12:9–10). It is Christ in me Who loves the man who cuts me off on the road. It is Christ in me Who says no to the temptations of the table. It is Christ in me Who answers gossip with a word of charity. It is Christ in me Who sees souls and persons, not objects to be used.

Daniel Mattson

Active Participation

A significant aspect of our Lord's miracles is the cooperation He requires of the people involved. Rarely does He heal someone without requiring something. He tells the paralytic to take up his mat and walk (Mt 9:1–8; Mk 2:1–12; Lk 5:17–26), the man with the withered hand to stretch it forth (Mt 12:9–14; Mk 3:1–6; Lk 6:6–11), and the man born blind to go and wash (Jn 9:1–41). Consider how His commands challenge these men. He requires them to do the very thing that their malady prevents, the very thing that frustrates, discourages, and shames them: to get up and walk, to stretch out the hand, etc. But in order to receive the miracle, they must trust the command—and try. Their trust in His command provides the proper disposition to receive His miracle. For divine work to be accomplished, human trust is required.

So it is, for example, with the ten lepers (Lk 17:11–19). Jesus does not heal them outright. He requires something of them: "Go and show yourselves to the priests" (Lk 17:14). Now, this seems an unreasonable command. Lepers were banished from the public and liturgical life of Israel. They were forbidden contact with anyone. More to the point, lepers could approach priests only if they were *already* healed, so that the priests could confirm the cleansing. But our Lord does not heal them first and then send them off. Rather, He commands the very thing that human wisdom would advise against: to go before there is any evidence of healing.

And yet the lepers set out on this seemingly ridiculous errand. They trust in His command, as absurd as it sounds, and they obey. Trusting that they will be healed, they go to show themselves to the priest. And because of their faith, they receive the miracle: "*[A]s they went* they were cleansed" (Lk 17:14; italics added). Our Lord Himself points out the relationship between their faith and His miracle. When the one leper returns to give thanks, Jesus says, "[Y]our faith has made you well" (Lk 17:19). What worked the miracle was not only our Lord's healing power, but also the leper's faith in action.

In this miracle and others our Lord manifests the pattern of salvation. God's grace does not work without our trust. He will not force reconciliation, healing, or holiness upon us. We must participate in the healing He desires to give. Imagine the lepers had refused our Lord's command. Imagine they said, "No. Heal us now before we go." Or, going further, imagine the man born blind resisted and obstinately refused to go and wash. Imagine when our Lord commanded him to get up and walk, the paralytic responded, "Make me."

Such refusals would be absurd. But no more so than when we, willfully or by neglect, refuse to cooperate with our Lord's grace—that is, when we ask Him for something but do not act in trust; when we receive the Eucharist and expect It to produce effects in us without our cooperation; when we attend Mass and expect to "get something out of it", although interiorly we are far away from the sacrifice of the altar; when we pray for help in marriage but do not avail ourselves of the natural and supernatural aids available.

If we ask our Lord for things, we should do so in trust, and act on those prayers in trust. Like the lepers, if we believe we have already received it, it will be ours (cf. Mk 11:24; Jn 14:13–14; 16:23).

All-Nighter

On the evening of March 24, 1522, Ignatius of Loyola went to the monastery of Montserrat to the shrine of the "Black Madonna" that had drawn pilgrims for centuries. There he spent the night in prayer, standing or kneeling, but never resting or relaxing. He remained vigilant. At dawn, having placed his sword and armor at the altar of our Lady, he put on a beggar's cloak and followed Christ. Such vigils, although foreign to us, were not uncommon in his day. And still now monks and nuns rise early to pray, and people remain in prayer before the Blessed Sacrament throughout the night. They are watching, remaining vigilant for the Lord.

"Blessed are those servants whom the master finds awake when he returns" (Lk 12:37; cf. Mt 24:42). What Ignatius did that night, we must do throughout our entire lives. Vigilance is essential to the Christian life. Indeed, the great enemy of faith is not persecution but slumber. The Church thrives under persecution. At those moments she sees her purpose more clearly and more perfectly resembles her

Spouse. Ease, comfort, and complacency—these threaten the Christian life far more than persecution. They breed a spiritual stupor, a dullness of soul, and a forgetfulness of the Lord's return.

We might speak of someone "losing his faith". But people do not lose their faith as they lose their glasses or car keys. Rather, they grow complacent and comfortable, tired and sleepy. They fall into a slumber and fail to form their lives by the faith. Even as they sleep, their faith is taken from them. "I was so full of sleep," Dante explains, "when I first left the way of truth behind."[4]

Against this spiritual stupor we should cultivate a vigilance of mind and heart. We must remain, first, "mentally awake" (as the Boy Scouts pledge). Many fail to guard their minds against the world's skepticism, cynicism, and doubt. They allow the world's pernicious theories to infiltrate their thoughts. Even as they might continue to practice the faith, they become intellectually sleepy. Their thinking becomes more and more formed by the world. Before they know it, they judge their faith in terms of the world, rather than the reverse.

Intellectual vigilance requires us to monitor closely what we listen to, read, and watch. All media communicates ideas. If we want our faith to remain intact, we must learn to filter out those ideas. But more importantly, we ought to seek out that media that places in our minds good thoughts and trains our thinking in keeping with the mind of the Church.

Second, we must maintain a vigilance of the heart. In the end, vigilance is a function of love. Because we love Christ, we remain wide-awake—"waiting in joyful hope", as is prayed at Mass—for His return. Consider the vigilance needed in marriage. If the spouses do not guard their hearts, their mutual affection will soon be lost. Infidelity and divorce do not just "happen". They occur when one or both of the spouses fail to keep the heart vigilant for the other. Something or someone slowly comes in between them. They find that their love has been defeated through a lack of vigilance.

In the same way, Christ's Bride must guard her heart and daily renew her devotion to Him. Just as spouses must remain vigilant, so also we must guard our hearts so that nothing and no one damages or robs our love for Christ. We do this most of all through a healthy

---

[4] Dante Alighieri, *Inferno*, canto 1, 10–11, trans. Anthony Esolen (New York: The Modern Library, 2002), 3.

prayer life, through vigilance of prayer. We cannot pray only when it comes easily and makes us feel good. As Ignatius' vigil reminds us, our prayer must continue when difficult and challenging. Christ calls us to remain wide-awake at midnight or before sunrise—that is, to pray even when it becomes difficult, inconvenient, or boring.

In the world's view, Ignatius would have been much better off praying during the day. And according to the world, we should relax and make ourselves at home. But we choose vigilance instead of comfort, so that at Christ's return we may find ourselves seated at His table and Him waiting on us.

Building and Battling

When God created Adam, He gave him a twofold task: to cultivate the Garden and to guard it (Gen 2:15). Unfortunately for us, his failure to do the second crippled his ability to complete the first. But this twofold task has continued for man, and especially for those in the Lord's service. The prophet Jeremiah's vocation contained something of both battle and cultivation, both "to pluck up and to break down, to destroy and to overthrow" and "to build and to plant" (Jer 1:10). When Nehemiah restored the walls of Jerusalem against her enemies, he trained the workers to build with one hand and hold a weapon with the other (Neh 4:11).

It should not surprise us, then, that when our Lord speaks about the cost of discipleship He does so in terms of building and battling (cf. Luke 14:25–33). To be a disciple of Christ means, first, to build something: "[W]hich of you, desiring to build a tower, does not first sit down and count the cost, whether he has enough to complete it?" (Lk 14:28). Scripture commentaries indicate that the tower in this case would have been for a vineyard, to help keep watch over the property. So there is a defensive purpose already for the tower. But the ultimate purpose is not defense. It is, rather, the cultivation and growth of something beautiful and pleasing.

Our attention should be first to the growth of Christ in our own souls. That life, planted within us at Baptism, requires our constant attention and care. We should be cultivating and building up that initial grace. We also have a construction project outside of us—to build up the Church and others. We should use our prayers, words, and actions as construction materials and tools for this building project. Thus Saint Paul exhorts us to edify our neighbor (Rom 15:2), to speak only what builds up (Eph 4:29), to "[l]et all things be done for edification" (1 Cor 14:26).

And yet, we must be willing to do battle as well. Our Lord also describes discipleship in terms of a "king, going to encounter another king in war" (Lk 14:31). We have enemies who threaten our construction project. Some enemies come at us from the outside—that is, the threats and temptations of the world. The forces of the world do not take kindly to our construction. We should have a healthy awareness of the constant battle between what Saint Augustine termed the City of God and the City of Man. But the more dangerous enemies come from the inside—namely, from our own vices. If we do not do battle with them, they can bring down the whole house. Indeed, these enemies pose the greater danger because they are the most immediate threat and require more courage to oppose.

To build and to battle—that is the Christian life, not two separate tasks as much as one task with two dimensions. We must unite both efforts. Those who try to build without battling will soon find their work undone. Those who battle without building leave no lasting legacy and indeed do the faith a disservice with a belligerent attitude.

And there is a hierarchy to these efforts. Building, ultimately, is the greater thing. We battle only because we need to, because sin has entered the world, has disturbed God's creation, and threatens our work. We build because the Lord has created us for that purpose. And our ultimate hope is to have rest from the battle, in that dwelling not made with hands, eternal in heaven (2 Cor 5:1).

Fearing Greatness

"Fear is the chief activator of our faults." This adage, sometimes attributed to Saint Teresa of Ávila and often used in twelve-step programs, touches on a profound truth: specifically, how we can be ruled by fear. It is not for nothing that a common phrase throughout the Scriptures is "Do not be afraid" (for example: Gen 15:1; 46:3; Jer 1:8; Is 7:4; 35:4; 41:10; Mt 1:20; Lk 8:50; Jn 6:20). Whether from our Lord Himself or from His angelic messengers, the exhortation touches on a basic reaction of our fallen human nature: to fear God. Indeed, this was the first reaction of fallen man: "I was afraid . . . and I hid myself" (Gen 3:10). Those first words of fallen man neatly summarize his behavior throughout the ages.

We can discern the presence of fear at the deepest root of every sin. Even in the sin of Adam we can perhaps detect the fear of missing out on becoming like a god if he did not eat of the tree. So also today, we commit sins of even the greatest gravity not out of malice but out of fear. We fear rejection, suffering, or pain, so we try to control our situation—and make a mess of it instead. Our anger and envy, for example, usually proceed from a fear of being less than others, of being passed over.

But the parable of the talents (Mt 25:14–30) shows how fear operates in another regard. The parable tells of three servants entrusted with talents: one with five, the second with two, and the third with only one. The first two servants invest their wealth and make a profit on what the master had given them. The third, however, buries his talent and therefore has no profit to show the master upon his return. It is thus a parable primarily about the failure to invest the gifts of God. But the servant's *motive* for hiding his talents is instructive: "I was afraid, and I went and hid your talent in the ground" (Mt 25:25).

In this case, fear prompts the servant to commit not a horrendous sin but a sin of omission, and for that reason the parable is even more instructive. The third servant did not steal from his master. He did not spend the talent on some immoral activity. He simply failed to invest what the master had given him—out of fear. This should prompt us to consider how fear keeps us from growing in the faith.

Our Lord calls each of us to greater devotion, intimacy, and holiness. Why do we not respond? Why do we bury the gifts of grace that He entrusts to us? What do we fear? Perhaps we fear failure, in which case we should meditate on the fact that if we die trying for heaven, we win. The saints had plenty of failures on their way to perfection. Indeed, perfection was not theirs until death. Perhaps we fear losing the kind of life we want, in which case we should meditate on God's goodness to us, that He desires something for us far exceeding what we can imagine. Perhaps we fear the effort needed, that it would disrupt an otherwise comfortable life. Ironically this often drives us to expend more energy avoiding the Lord and burying our gifts than simple outright generosity would demand.

In the end, it is a failure of love, a failure to think first of God, that leads to fear. "[P]erfect love casts out fear" (1 Jn 4:18), because when we enter into that relationship of love with the Father, we realize that we have nothing to fear in our feeble, repeated attempts to serve Him. He is patient with His children and delights in their efforts. We should not bury our gifts out of fear but invest them in full confidence that our heavenly Father delights in even the smallest effort to bear fruit.

Unprofitable Servants Profiting

What to do when Bible passages seem to contradict one another? Critics of Christianity might just shrug and conclude that all of Scripture is just a jumble of contradictions anyway. Believers, of course, should not trivialize the difficulty of squaring one text with another. But neither should we think that they cannot be explained. In fact, reflecting and meditating on such seeming contradictions often bears great spiritual fruit.

Take, for example, two different parables. In that of the unprofitable servants, the master welcomes his servant not by saying, "Come here immediately and take your place at table," but rather, "Prepare supper for me, and put on your apron and serve me, till I eat and drink; and afterward you shall eat and drink" (Lk 17:8). Now this seems to run afoul of another parable, also about faithful servants, in which the master will in fact "put on his apron and have them sit at table, and he will come and serve them" (Lk 12:37).

So, which one is it? Will the servants do the serving or be served? Do these parables contradict each other? Or is there another way of looking at them? Indeed, if we trust in the divine Author's integrity, then we will see that these passages do not contradict but complement each another.

First, the parable of the unprofitable servants teaches our basic status before the Lord. We are ever dependent on Him. We must therefore be, as He commands, poor in spirit; that is, we must acknowledge that we have nothing of our own to contribute. No amount of service or fidelity empowers us to make a claim on Him for anything. If we are faithful, it is only what we are supposed to do, and we can only do it because of His grace. So He reasonably commands us to say, "We are unworthy servants; we have only done what was our duty" (Lk 17:10).

The severity of these words shocks us into remembering what we so often forget: He is God; we are not—He owes us nothing; we owe Him everything. It is strong medicine against our entitlement mentality. We tend to reverse the order and think that we have put God in our debt. We then resent Him when life does not go as we think it should. The parable and its conclusion jerk us back to the right path of spiritual poverty.

Now if the lesson of the unprofitable servants emphasizes our poverty before God, then the parable of the vigilant stewards highlights God's generosity toward us. He pledges to reward His faithful by girding Himself as a servant and treating them as special guests. We have a right to nothing from Him—and yet He promises everything.

More to the point, His liberality depends on our poverty. It ceases to be generosity once we have a right to it. And the more we realize that we are paupers, the greater His generosity appears. Only when we first understand our nothingness can we then appreciate His liberality. Only when we understand our sinfulness can we understand His mercy.

So these two parables support one another in revealing our poverty and God's generosity. Without a strong sense of our nothingness, we run headlong into presumption and entitlement—that most obnoxious of vices, characteristic of the Pharisees. At the same time, without trust in God's mercy, we fall into despair—that most debilitating spiritual malady. A strong sense of both helps us appreciate the greatness of our faith: that to us who have no claim on Him, God has indebted Himself.

Unilateral Forgiveness

Jesus said to the woman, "Your sins are forgiven" (Lk 7:48). What beautiful words from our Savior to this sinful woman. What a wonderful act of forgiveness and mercy. The only problem is, she had not asked for it. In fact, no one in the gospels asks for His forgiveness—not the paralytic lowered through the roof for healing, not the jeering crowd on Calvary. Yet He forgives them anyway. This woman, by her gestures of repentance—bathing His feet with tears, drying them with her hair, and anointing them with oil—comes the closest. Her actions speak what she in fact never says: "Forgive me."

All of this emphasizes God's initiative: He forgives before we ask. He bestows mercy even though we are unworthy of it. He does not require that we be perfect in order to be forgiven—that would be a contradiction. He does not insist that we ask in just the right way—with all our i's dotted and t's crossed. That would amount to Christian reincarnation: keep trying until you get it right. No, He extends forgiveness before we are ready, before we even ask. So, when we ask for forgiveness, we are not trying to change His mind, as if He has to be cajoled and persuaded. Rather, we are availing ourselves of something already extended to us. We ask for His forgiveness, not so that He will give it (for He already has), but so that we can receive it.

This should give us confidence in approaching the Sacrament of Penance. Forgiveness awaits us there already. We enter the confessional not to convince the minister to forgive but to avail ourselves of what he is there to give. The requirements for a good confession (examine the conscience, make a firm purpose of amendment, list the sins clearly and do not withhold mortal sins) are not tests or hurdles, but how we open the soul to receive forgiveness. And even after all that, no one can say he confessed *perfectly*. No human act of repentance can sufficiently express the gravity of sin or make one worthy of mercy. So, like the woman in the Gospel, we sort of barge into the confessional and awkwardly but sincerely give expression *as best we can* to our sorrow for sin and desire for reconciliation. Forgiveness awaits us in the confessional. We simply need to avail ourselves of it.

Our Lord's initiative in forgiveness, His unilateral decision to forgive before anyone asks, should likewise shape our mercy toward others. We pray daily for a correspondence between God's mercy and ours: "Forgive us our trespasses as we forgive those who trespass against us." God extends forgiveness before we are worthy—before we even ask. We, however, hold grudges and say, "I will forgive so-and-so when he comes and asks." Or, "I will forgive her when she shows me she is sorry." What if God did that? What if He withheld His mercy until we had performed some act worthy of it? We approach Him in confidence precisely because we know that He forgives despite our unworthiness. Others should feel the same freedom with us.

This is what it means to love one's enemies—to make the interior decision to forgive, whether or not the other asks for our forgiveness. The day may come when the person asks, in which case we can be reconciled. In other situations, sadly, that day may never come, in which case we imitate our Lord even more by bearing in our hearts forgiveness for those who have not asked. Christian forgiveness goes forth before the offender has repented, despite his unworthiness. That is how Christ acts toward us, and how we ought to act toward others.

Trusting and Transformed

"Follow me, and I will make you fishers of men" (Mt 4:19; cf. Mk 1:17). By these simple words our Lord calls the Apostles Peter and Andrew, James and John. Obviously, the words have a unique meaning for them and likewise a particular meaning for all priests. But they apply also in a broader way to everyone. The experience of the Apostles is in a sense normative for all in the apostolic Church. Christ's call of them sets the pattern for how He calls us now.

First there is the centrality of Jesus. His call of the Apostles has two parts: a summons ("Follow me") and a promise ("I will make you ..."). Jesus is precisely at the center of the phrases ("me", "I"). He is the One to follow. He is the One Who transforms. He does not call us to an idea or a theory. He does not invite us to a hypothesis. He calls us to Himself and to His transforming power.

Thus the response to the call is a response to Jesus Himself, to His beauty and goodness. He is not just a man but the perfect man. Certainly He had no sin. But neither did He have any foibles, quirks, or off-putting habits. His noble and good character was literally attractive—drawing people after Him. So attractive, in fact, that these fishermen—hardworking, practical-minded men—left everything behind and followed Him, to they knew not where. This brings us to another element of the call.

Trust. "Follow me," Jesus says to the Apostles. And nothing more. No indication about the route, destination, or purpose. Soon they will witness exorcisms and dramatic healings. They will become embroiled in controversy with their religious leaders. They will go up to Jerusalem and see Him hailed one day, crucified another. They will see Him risen from the dead and will preach His Gospel to the ends of the earth. But now that is hidden from their eyes. All they see is the Man before them. And that is enough. "Follow me," He says. It is not knowledge of what will happen that prompts the Apostles to follow. It is trust in Him.

God does not show us the plan from beginning to end. He does not give us the itinerary in advance. He asks us to trust. We want to know everything ahead of time, to see every last detail before we set out. "Where are we going? What should I bring? What will I do? Will I be happy?" But the Apostles show the proper response. The itinerary did not matter as much as the Companion. The destination did not matter as long as He was with them on the journey. And that journey was more profoundly interior than external. This brings us to the final point.

Transformation. Our Lord promises nothing to the Apostles except what He will do to them: "I will make you fishers of men." He does not promise wealth or fame or pleasure. He does not even guarantee success in their work. He promises only to make them more than they are. And He was faithful to that promise, making these simple fishermen the foundation of His Church.

God calls us in order to transform us. Yes, He calls us to certain tasks. But external success in accomplishing a task is not as important as allowing His grace to work within us. If God has called us to a particular work or state in life, it is not so that we will simply do the work (after all, He could do it better Himself), but so that we will be transformed (sanctified) in our labor for Him.

It is by way of trust in Jesus Christ that we are transformed. The transformation comes by way of the following. We think (and insist) that He will transform us in order to follow Him. But it works the other way. He calls us—like the Apostles, imperfect and unprepared—to trust in Him personally. He will do the rest, transforming us according to our trust.

Wait—Just Wait

The Israelites could not wait any longer. Moses showed no sign of returning from the mountaintop any time soon. So they took things into their own hands. They cajoled Aaron into fashioning a golden calf for them to worship. Thus they swiftly left the way of the Lord and fell into idolatry (Ex 32:1–6). Fast-forward some years. Saul showed a similar impatience with Samuel, the Lord's prophet. Not knowing the time of Samuel's return, he decided to do things on his own. And that was the beginning of the end for him (1 Sam 13:2–14).

Perhaps our Lord has these examples in mind when he describes the unfaithful steward's thoughts: "My master is delayed in coming" (Lk 12:45). That steward falls into the same error as the Israelites, Saul, and countless others. He grows impatient with the master's seeming delay. At the heart of infidelity is this impatience—an unwillingness to wait for the Lord.

Some of us are more impatient than others. But impatience is deep within us all. Indeed, we can interpret Original Sin in this light. It can be seen as the desire to possess immediately—to grasp for—what God intended to give. Ever since that first sin, our fallen human nature has this tragic inclination to seek the immediate possession of things. Our technological society only exacerbates this wound. We grow accustomed to instantaneous responses and results. Every business and company caters to this, promising us prompt service, immediate results, etc. No waiting.

How different is the life of faith. It requires patience and waiting. As Pope Francis says in *Lumen Fidei*: "Faith by its very nature demands renouncing the immediate possession which sight would appear to offer."[5] Scripture often gives voice to this truth with the plaintive yet faithful plea, "How long, O LORD?" (Ps 13:1; 35:17; cf. 6:3; Hab 1:2). The initiative always belongs to God. Faith requires us to wait on Him, to allow Him to make Himself known. We operate according to His schedule, not our own. And if He seems to delay, we do not take things into our own hands.

The refusal to wait—that impatient grasping for control—leads us into sin. With the Israelites it took the form of idolatry. Not willing to wait for the Lord, they fashioned a god for themselves. At the heart of idolatry lurks impatience with God. When we grow tired of waiting for Him, we begin to create our own gods—perhaps not graven images, but certainly our own little interests, ideologies, and activities that eclipse Him in our hearts.

And such impatience leads swiftly to other sins—because morality requires patience. So, after worshipping the golden calf, the Israelites "sat down to eat and drink, and rose up to play [a euphemism, to be sure]" (Ex 32:6). And the unfaithful steward begins "to beat the menservants and the maidservants, and to eat and drink and get drunk" (Lk 12:45).

Each of us has experienced this impatience. When will God answer my prayers? How much longer must I keep going? Where is He? And yet, as dangerous as that impatience may be, it can become an occasion to increase in our desire to see Him and to experience His power. In this regard we have the example of our Lord Himself longing for the fulfillment of His mission: "I came to cast fire upon the earth; and would that it were already kindled! I have a baptism to be baptized with; and how I am constrained until it is accomplished!" (Lk 12:49–50). We also have the example of our Lady, waiting patiently on Holy Saturday for God's power, so hidden from the world, to be revealed. May we show our faith similarly, submitting our impatience to His grace, that it may become a holy longing.

[5] Pope Francis, Encyclical Letter *Lumen Fidei*, June 29, 2013, no. 13, http://w2.vatican.va /content/francesco/en/encyclicals/documents/papa-francesco_20130629_enciclica-lumen -fidei.html.

What a Shame

Mark Twain once quipped, "Man is the only Animal that Blushes. He is the only one that has occasion to."[6] He may have intended this only as a comment on man's immorality. But, perhaps inadvertently, he also pointed to man's dignity. Man's ability to blush—his shame—comes not just from his wrongdoing but, more importantly, from his recognition of it. We blush because, unlike the other animals, we are moral agents capable of virtue, vice—and repentance. Man's dignity causes him to blush. If we had no dignity, we would have no shame.

Shame and dignity work together to cause the prodigal son's conversion. Working among swine and starving to the point that he "would gladly have fed on the pods on which the swine ate" (Lk 15:16), he saw the shameful depravity of his sins. Perhaps he even blushed. "But when he came to himself" (Lk 15:17), he realized that, although his sins had reduced him to the level of the animals, he still maintained a certain dignity. He realized the truth of himself, of his own worth, and also of his ability to repent. "[H]e arose and came to his father" (Lk 15:20).

As with the prodigal son, so also with us: shame reminds us of our dignity. It comes about when our conscience accuses us of sin and reveals that certain thoughts, words, or actions contradict our status as children of God. It is the moral nervous system alerting us of injury. Shame shows us the depravity of our sins and the need to repent. Notice that proper shame is directed toward our sins, not toward ourselves. It highlights the disconnect between our dignity and our behavior. And it thus enables us to "come to our senses"—better, to return to ourselves—and then return to our heavenly Father. Without shame, there can be no repentance. Therefore the ability to be ashamed is a sign of moral health. And a society that cannot blush, such as our own, is in moral free fall.

Indeed, as painful as shame can be, there is something worse: the silent conscience that fails to accuse and produces no shame. Such a

[6] Mark Twain, "The Lowest Animal", *Letters from Earth*, ed. Bernard DeVoto (New York: Harper & Row, 1962), 236.

conscience allows us to continue in sin. It is the failure of the moral nervous system. It produces men who cannot recognize good and evil, virtue and vice, morality and immorality, men who think they are "persons who need no repentance" (Lk 15:7). Pope Pius XII said, "The gravest threat to the soul comes not from shame or even from sin, but from what Pope Pius XII called the greatest sin of the world today—the loss of the sense of sin."[7]

If shame reminds us of our dignity, repentance restores it. In shame, the prodigal son confessed his sins: "Father, I have sinned against heaven and before you; I am no longer worthy to be called your son" (Lk 15:18–19). In repentance, he received back what he had lost—his status as the father's son. Upon seeing his shame and repentance, the father "had compassion, and ran and embraced him and kissed him" (Lk 15:20). We ought to enter the confessional like the prodigal son, carrying not just shame for our sins, but also confidence in the restoration of our status as children of God.

In fact, repentance not only confirms our dignity—it enhances it. The father did not forgive his son begrudgingly. Nor did he ridicule or belittle him. On the contrary, he granted him more far more than the son expected: the finest robe, a ring on his finger, sandals on his feet, and the fattened calf (Lk 15:22–23). We receive far greater gifts than these, and far more than we deserve, when we go to confession. We encounter the true Father in the confessional, where we kneel shameful and repentant to rise forgiven and restored.

In fact, the glory of the confessional reaches all the way to heaven, where there will be "joy before the angels of God over one sinner who repents" (Lk 15:10). And if the heavenly host sees fit to rejoice, what a shame if we did not join in.

[7] Pius XII, Radio Message of His Holiness Pius XII to Participants in the National Catechetical Congress of the United States in Boston, Pontifical Palace in Castel Gondolfo, October 26, 1946, https://w2.vatican.va/content/pius-xii/en/speeches/1946/documents/hf _p-xii_spe_19461026_congresso-catechistico-naz.html.

IX

FEASTS

The Pattern and Rhythm of the Christian Life

Introduction

by Raymond Arroyo

In my hometown of New Orleans, every day is a celebration: a cas-
cade of feast days marking grace-filled moments in our shared history. The locals don't observe these occasions coldly; they experience
them anew, each year, in grand style. This is as it should be.

Unlike the rest of the country, owing to its still vibrant Catholic
culture, New Orleans marks time by its feasts. Sit in a Magazine
Street coffee shop long enough and you're likely to hear, "Why don't
we try to get together right after the Epiphany? But, please, don't forget to remind me. Otherwise, we'll be in the middle of the Carnival
season, and then I won't have no time."

The great Southern novelist Walker Percy once wrote about the
intoxicating "liturgical rhythm" of New Orleans. It is hard not to get
swept up in that distinctively Catholic tempo, whether one happens
to be Catholic or not. All are welcome and all are needed. In truth,
most people come for the party and the food, but they stay for the
mystery and the truth behind it, if it is shared with them. This is as
it should be.

A part of me aches for those outside the Crescent City who have
never experienced a faith fully lived by an entire community. Native
New Orleanians learn pretty early that faith, if it is to thrive and

spread, cannot be confined to the shadows. It is a thing in need of public expressions.

My eyes often go glassy when people begin to prattle on about "the new evangelization". Too often, what follows is a clinical checklist of what should be done to attract others to their otherwise unattractive faith. What the world craves are inviting displays of faith, and New Orleans does that better than most. For a graduate course in "the new evangelization", take a trip down to NOLA during a major feast day.

Nowhere are so many specialty foods, parades, and festivals created—by such diverse people—to commemorate sacred mysteries and the feast days of beloved saints. If you want to feel Lent in all its profundity, come visit at the start of the Carnival season and stay past Fat Tuesday. After twelve days of Christmas and the explosive party that is Mardi Gras (our Lenten prep), Ash Wednesday lands with a thud. The deprivation can be felt viscerally. It's as if you have been speeding along at three hundred miles an hour when suddenly someone throws the brakes on. The rollicking balls, the rich foods, and the family parades stop instantly, and the long climb to Easter begins with only Saint Joseph and Saint Patrick to ease the passage.

Saint Joseph's Day is a wonderful example of a feast day in practice. Following the Sicilian tradition, generations of New Orleanians have saluted Jesus' father by erecting Saint Joseph altars all over town. Proscribed breads, cookies, and fish cover multitiered tables built in homes and schools, restaurants, or churches. There is no meat on the altars since the feast day falls during Lent. Neighbors and friends are invited to pray around the sacred tables as they are blessed by priests. Usually during the blessing, children dressed as the Holy Family knock at two doors in the neighborhood. They are turned away at each stop. Finally they come to the altar site where the "Holy Family" are welcomed in and fed. The host family literally welcomes Joseph, Mary, and the baby Jesus to their food-laden table. Soon all are invited to feast on the pasta and fish and sweets. Those who maintain the tradition each year tell me they offer the expense and the laborious food preparation to Saint Joseph in thanksgiving for his intercession or as a lavish petition for his assistance. For anyone gathered at a Saint Joseph altar, the senses are fully engaged. The faith is suddenly made tangible—they can see and taste it—and the saint is made accessible in a whole new way. Thousands participate in such celebrations throughout the year. This is as it should be.

Before you think that this is some crass advertisement for the New Orleans Tourism Commission, my point is this: no matter where we find ourselves, every local parish and home has the possibility of living our feast days in a more expressive and inclusive way. Through a more intentional public display, these precious days are enlarged and incarnate the occasion of wonder or the life of sanctity recalled. The day becomes something interactive and a public vehicle of grace.

An image from my childhood comes to mind. It is of a Corpus Christi procession through the French Quarter around the St. Louis Cathedral. It is probably Archbishop Philip Hannan carrying Christ in the monstrance to a people sorely in need of His presence. Acolytes and canopy bearers move solemnly past bars and jazz joints. Scantily clad, bruised-up women in doorways kneel as He passes. A woozy guy sitting on the curb drops his cigarette into a go cup and crosses himself. Once again that eternal clash of the sacred and the profane that the rest of the world tries to ignore or deny is made manifest. This is what feast days are all about: dedicated times for us to stop and experience the deeper spiritual reality beyond the blur of our chaotic lives.

Here's hoping that the following will lead you and yours to live each feast day to the fullest—as they should be lived.

Raymond Arroyo

The Paradox of Christmas

With Christmas we celebrate one of the Church's most beautiful and most important paradoxes—indeed, the one that gives meaning to so many others—namely, the astounding truth that the infinite, immortal, all-powerful God is born of the Virgin Mary as a small, mortal, defenseless baby. It is a foundational truth of Christianity that the Child in Bethlehem is fully human and fully divine.

To get this wrong means to cease being Christian. And history displays the many different ways people have gone wrong. The Church has heard all the heretical claims: Jesus is part God and part man; He is a divine Person and a human person somehow sharing the same body; He is God pretending to be a man; He is a man who somehow became God. And so on. To all these the Church responds with the true and saving doctrine of the Incarnation: Jesus, the eternal Son of God, from the moment of His conception in Mary's womb, is true God and true man, fully human and fully divine. It is God's own birth we celebrate.

Although we confess this truth every Sunday, perhaps we do not fully interiorize it. Perhaps there still lingers within us, not so much the thought, but the *suspicion* or the *sense* that through it all God is playacting, that he sort of dressed up in a human outfit for a while the way we may put on a costume. Or maybe we think that the Son of God made the choice at one moment to become man, and the rest was beyond his control, just the consequences of His decision. Because the truth is so difficult to grasp and the errors so easy to fall into, we must remind ourselves that at every moment of His life the eternal Son of God was *choosing* to be human and to experience our human condition fully—with all its limitations, frailties, and weaknesses. He did not just pretend to be an infant but chose at every moment of His infant life to be small, helpless, and fragile.

Further, as we look upon the baby Jesus in the manger, we should not think that His Incarnation is simply God becoming small *although* He is almighty, or because He is omnipotent He begrudgingly endures being small. On the contrary, God reveals His power most especially in His capacity to become small. The smallness and weakness of the infant does not violate but fully expresses God's almighty power. We can understand this truth by way of the words of Saint Francis de Sales: "Nothing is so strong as gentleness, nothing so gentle as real strength."[1] Indeed, we touch on this truth with the colloquialism (now used more often cynically than sincerely) that it is "big" of a man to perform some unnecessary kindness or to show someone mercy.

Thus, unlike the Islamic god whose power is made known only by way of his infinite distance and his imperious commands, the Triune God of Christianity displays His grandeur and glory by drawing near to us in the Person of the Son. He reveals the power that created the world, most of all by entering that world as a child. His greatness is in His capacity to be merciful, gentle, small, and near to us.

We should approach our Lord in a manner that corresponds to His Incarnation. The entrance of the Mighty One as a child should banish from our hearts any servile fear. He appeals to us from the crib, assuring us that He comes not to compel us or overwhelm us—but rather to use His strength for our salvation, His power for our healing.

Incarnate Love

Just for fun, the next time you hear people refer to the "Christmas spirit" or the "spirit of Christmas", ask them what they mean. By "spirit" they usually mean a vague attitude or a warm feeling surrounding a holiday that falls in an otherwise grim time of year. Rarely if ever does this "spirit" refer to anything specific or concrete—which makes it the very antithesis of Christmas, because Christmas is about something amazingly and gloriously concrete, specific, and particular: the birth of Christ.

"And the Word became flesh and dwelt among us" (Jn 1:14). The One Who dwells in inapproachable light became visible. God Himself took on our human nature and was born of the Virgin Mary—in a specific place and at a particular time. He lived and worked among us, shared our joys and took on our suffering. He spoke to us

[1] Pierre Camus, *The Spirit of Saint Francis DeSales* (London: Longmans, Green, 1921), 11.

directly—spoke specific words with certain meaning. He offered His life as the definitive sign of His love. Now we know His love as a concrete and tangible reality. His love is not just a concept or a theory; it is as real and living as the Baby in the manger.

By His birth, our Lord teaches us this truth: love seeks to be concrete. We cannot love in a general sort of way. Rather, true love expresses itself in concrete ways and toward particular persons. No lover is ever satisfied with a fuzzy feeling of affection for his beloved. He wants to display his love by specific acts that can be seen, heard, and felt. So he calls her on the phone, sends cards, brings flowers, gives her a kiss, embraces her. It is not enough for him to say, "I love you." His words must become flesh.

For some, the particularity of love might cut too close to the bone. We may regard God's love as a nice idea, a wonderful notion—provided He makes no demands. As long as He stays up above and does not interfere, we rejoice in His vague, unobtrusive love. But if He comes to us and makes His love visible and concrete, we may have to respond. We may have to change. So we dodge the specifics and talk instead about the "Christmas spirit". But we never allow that spirit to become flesh.

The same danger exists with human love. It is a demanding thing to love specific, particular persons. They can be so uncooperative—they may reject us. We find it easier to keep our love for others vague, to keep love of neighbor on the level of an idea and never display it by concrete acts of love. And so we are tempted to pay lip service to love, but never allow it to become flesh in our lives.

"And the Word became flesh and dwelt among us." God's love for us became flesh, even a child—someone we can see, hear, and touch. By this He sets the standard for all love. And it is fitting that a child should challenge us in this way. With every new child in a family, the husband and wife give a concrete, specific, living, breathing expression of their love. Their love truly becomes flesh. (And what is contraception but a couple's way of saying, "Our love will not become flesh"?)

So we return to the manger and allow the Christ child to instruct us. He silently but powerfully appeals to us—teaching us by His very presence that the prodigal love of the Father is real, is present, and has come into the world for the salvation of our souls. "In this way the love of God was made manifest among us, that God sent his only-begotten Son into the world, so that we might live through him" (1 Jn 4:9).

Keeping Appointments

Have you ever missed an appointment? There is that awful feeling of having inconvenienced someone, let someone down, and missed an opportunity. Perhaps that painful experience can give us a hint of what happened upon the magi's arrival in Jerusalem. And perhaps it can keep us from missing appointments in the future.

When they arrive in Jerusalem, the magi ask, " 'Where is he who has been born king of the Jews? For we have seen his star in the East, and have come to worship him.' When Herod the king heard this, he was troubled, and all Jerusalem with him" (Mt 2:2–3). Now, we can understand why the magi's question would trouble King Herod. He did not like the news of another king, a competitor. But why would it trouble "all Jerusalem"? Why would the news of a king's birth upset them? Simply put, because they realized that they had missed an appointment—indeed, *the* appointment.

The Israelites were people of waiting—"prisoners of hope", as one prophet calls them (Zech 9:12). Their identity rested on the promise of the Messiah, the King Who was to come. They all, individually and as a nation, looked for His coming. Their prophets had promised Him and told them what to look for. And now these magi—these foreigners—arrive in the capital and announce that the long-awaited One has been born. And all Jerusalem is troubled because they missed it. The Messiah is born, and they have missed the appointment.

It is a cautionary tale, of course. The negligence and complacency of the chief priests and scribes is a warning to us. Like them, we are blessed with many promises of our Lord. We have Scripture, the sacraments, indeed Christ's abiding presence in the Church herself. And He has established appointments with us. He has promised to come to us at certain times: in Mass, in confession, in prayer, etc. In fact, He promised to abide within us permanently.

Like the leaders of Israel, we run the risk of becoming so familiar with the promises that we neglect them, get distracted—and fail to keep the appointments. The leaders of Israel were complacent because they were comfortable. They had established for themselves a livable situation with the Romans. Their power and authority in Israel were secure. They had found their way in the world—or, rather, the world had found its way in them (as C.S. Lewis quips[2]). Even Herod's unsolicited question about the birthplace of the Messiah cannot rouse them from their complacency. And this again serves as a warning to us Catholics. When we grow comfortable in the world, then we neglect our Lord's presence and we begin to miss appointments. Indeed, history bears witness to the Gospel paradox again and again: we are more faithful when we are uncomfortable and at odds with the world.

This scene is about evangelization as well. Nonbelievers arrive in Jerusalem seeking the one true God. But His own people cannot bear witness to Him. Because they have grown comfortable in the world, they have nothing to offer the world. May we, who enjoy the Messiah's abiding presence, be able to answer confidently and joyfully when those seeking the truth come to us and say, in effect, "Where is he who has been born king of the Jews? For we have seen his star in the East, and have come to worship him."

His Transfiguration, and Ours

When we encounter Jesus Christ, we encounter ourselves—ourselves, that is, not as we are but as we are to become. Vatican II's *Gaudium et Spes*, in its most famous passage, states that "Christ ... fully reveals man to man himself". His words and actions are normative. They reveal to us how to live an authentically human life. The sentence continues by stating that Jesus "makes his supreme calling clear".[3]

---

[2] C. S. Lewis, *The Screwtape Letters* (New York: Macmillan, 1982), 132.

[3] Vatican Council II, Pastoral Constitution on the Church in the Modern World, *Gaudium et Spes*, December 7, 1965, no. 22, http://w2.vatican.va/content/john-paul-ii/en/encyclicals/documents/hf_jp-ii_enc_04031979_redemptor-hominis.html#%241S.

Jesus, in revealing His own glory, reveals also the glory that is to be ours.

So it is at the Transfiguration (Mt 17:1–13; Mk 9:2–8; Lk 9:28–36). The Apostles, privileged to witness that event, certainly knew our Lord better as a result. The human veil over His divinity was for a moment lifted, and they beheld His heavenly splendor. John would write years later, "[W]e have beheld his glory, glory as of the only-begotten Son from the Father" (Jn 1:14). And so also Peter: "[W]e were eyewitnesses of his majesty" (2 Pet 1:16).

But not only *His* glory and majesty—they also beheld the "upward call" of every Christian. To behold Christ in glory is to behold our final end. Saint Augustine says that the transfigured Christ reveals what His Body is to become.[4] We are to be transfigured as well. The purpose of everything in our faith—of all doctrines and sacraments—is to change us "from one degree of glory to another" (2 Cor 3:18).

Peter intuits this call and thus desires to remain on Mount Tabor, in the presence of the transfigured Christ: "Lord, it is well that we are here; if you wish, I will make three booths here" (Mt 17:4; cf. Mk 9:5; Lk 9:33). Perhaps Peter's words are ill-timed. But his response shows how the human heart *ought* to respond in the light of Christ's glory: "This is what I have always desired.... I was created for this.... I want to remain in this presence. To behold is to be held."

Further, ours is to be not only the glory of Christ but also the testimony of the Father. We are to hear the words of the Father applied to ourselves: "This is my beloved Son, with whom I am well pleased" (Mt 17:5; cf. Mk 9:7; Lk 9:35). Again, the entire Christian life can be understood as the progressive knowing of ourselves as the Father's beloved children. "This is my beloved Son, with whom I am well pleased." The project of the Christian life is to train our ears to hear these words and our hearts to accept them.

And yet in this encounter Peter also receives what appears to be a rebuke: "He was still speaking, when behold, a bright cloud overshadowed them, and a voice from the cloud said, 'This is my beloved Son, with whom I am well pleased; listen to him'" (Mt 17:5; cf. Mk 9:7; Lk 9:35). "Listen to him" is an odd command at the Transfiguration. The event involves sight, not hearing. We would expect "*Look* at him." Why then the command to listen?

---

[4] Saint Augustine, Exposition on Psalm 50, 12; see also *CCC* 556.

We can take "Listen to him" in the broadest sense: we ought to heed Jesus' every word. But in the context of the Transfiguration this command refers to our Lord's Passion. The journey up the mountain had followed Jesus' first prophecy of His Passion: "Jesus began to show his disciples that he must go to Jerusalem and suffer many things from the elders and chief priests and scribes, and be killed, and on the third day be raised" (Mt 16:21; cf. Mk 8:31; Lk 9:22). The Apostles—and especially Peter—had received this poorly. Worse still, Jesus then spoke about the need to follow Him in this suffering: "If any man would come after me, let him deny himself and take up his cross and follow me. For whoever would save his life will lose it, and whoever loses his life for my sake will find it" (Mt 16:24–25; cf. 10:38–39; Lk 14:27; 17:33; Jn 12:25). It was hard to listen to these words.

Now, at the Transfiguration, the Father's voice resounds to confirm what the Son had said: "Listen to him." Peter, who wants so much to remain on the mountain, must first learn the path of the Passion. It is a command to believe Jesus' words not only about His own death and Resurrection but also about our need to follow Him. Jesus is transfigured to reveal the final goal: glory. The Father's voice is heard to highlight the means to that end: the Cross. "Listen to him," because the Passion is the path to glory. That He shares with us the glory of His Transfiguration means also that we must share in His Passion.

To encounter Christ is to encounter ourselves. When we behold His glory, we learn our lofty calling and goal. When we listen to His words, we learn the path to such glory. "The truth is that only in the mystery of the incarnate Word does the mystery of man take on light."[5]

"Fearful yet Overjoyed"

It's a curious thing that a father does. The same child that he protects and cradles, he takes in his hands and throws into the air, up above his head, lets him fall back, and then catches again. And again throws him, lets him fall, and catches him. It seems odd to do to a child. But

[5] *Gaudium et Spes*, no. 22.

watch. The child laughs and even shrieks with delight. He screams in midflight and giggles when caught.

There is fear of being in the air, without support, helpless and not in control. There is fear of being so dependent on this big man. But then there is the joy of being received back into his arms and brought close to him again. All one fluid motion, the throwing and the catching. Which means that the fear and the joy are united as well. "Then they went away quickly from the tomb, fearful yet overjoyed, and ran to announce this to his disciples" (Mt 28:8, NABRE). This description of the women on Easter Sunday resembles the fear and joy that the child experiences in his father's arms. As in that experience, the fear and joy in this instance are united, one being impossible without the other.

The fear of the women is, of course, the reverence that we call fear of the Lord. They just encountered the angel and received news of something beyond their control. Christ is risen. No human intellect can make sense of it; no human power can tame it. The women are reminded powerfully of that fundamental truth: He is God and we are not. Their smallness—and ours—is evident.

In His Resurrection appearances, Jesus always teaches the transcendence and otherness that elicits fear. He cannot be controlled. He is master of the situation, remaining for a time unrecognizable to Mary Magdalene, the disciples on the road, the Apostles in the boat—revealing Himself only on His own terms. He suddenly disappears in Emmaus. And just as suddenly He appears before the Apostles. The Lord rebukes the two people—Mary Magdalene and Thomas—who try to have Him on their own terms. The risen Christ will not be domesticated. He must be feared in order to be received. Only when that fear is present can joy arise.

Easter joy is not something manufactured or created by us. It comes from the Resurrection or not at all, precisely and only when we surrender control and allow the risen Lord to intrude on our gatherings and activities just as surely as He appeared on the road, in the upper room, and on the seashore. If we want Him on our own terms—and thus without fear—then it is not the risen Lord we want, but a caricature.

Fear and joy seem always to have been together, or at least meant to be. Adam's joy depended on a healthy reverence for that one prohibition and the ominous warning: lest you die. When he and

Eve reached out to grasp—that is, to control God's arrangement, to define their own reality—at that very moment their joy was lost. They even hid from God. Since that moment, we children of Adam have suffered the deep, sinful inclination to wrest control from God, for ourselves. We are constantly grasping for joy on our own terms and, therefore, always losing it.

This is at the core of sin, to prefer our reality to God's, to seek joy on our own terms. Such has always been the case. But this is also a timely consideration, because we live in an irreverent and therefore a joyless culture. We lack fear of the Lord and consequently lack authentic joy, settling for pleasure as a cheap imitation.

This matter of fear of the Lord—whether we are reverent or irreverent—determines how we view the world. In short, reality is either given and received, or invented and imposed. By fear of the Lord, we receive the reality of which God Himself is the Author. We conform ourselves to the Author's will and plot line. By our irreverence, however, we invent our own reality and impose it on others. These fault lines lie in every human heart. But as much as every human heart may struggle, in the past there was at least general agreement that reality is not something we invent but something given to us and received. Now, however, the invention of reality is not only possible, but essential to society. The Supreme Court has even codified our impiety and irreverence: "At the heart of liberty is the right to define one's own concept of existence, of meaning, of the universe, and of the mystery of human life."[6] An invented reality, having no objective truth, cannot be agreed upon. It must be imposed.

Indeed, these fault lines—given and received, invented, and imposed—are writ large in society. They characterize all our debates: about sex, sexuality, marriage, law, and even liturgy. Either we receive the given truth of these and find joy therein, or we make it up and force others to come along. Technology exacerbates the problem, making us feel like masters of time and space, thus having the authority and power to define existence, meaning, universe, and life.

"Fearful yet overjoyed." This describes those first messengers of the Resurrection, the first Christian witnesses. So also should it

---

[6] *Planned Parenthood of Southeastern Pennsylvania et al. v. Casey, Governor of Pennsylvania, et al.*, 505 U.S. 833 (1992).

describe Christians today. The world cries out for such witnesses, for those who joyfully point beyond this world to eternal truths. We ought, then, to be fearful—acknowledging our smallness, our absolute dependence on the Author of life and the reality of His creation. And precisely because of that holy fear we should also be found joyful—ever rejoicing in what He has done for us, in being caught once more and gathered to His bosom.

Four Gardens

"Mary Magdalene came to the tomb early, while it was still dark" (Jn 20:1; cf. Mt 28:1; Mk 16:1–2; Lk 24:1). She comes to a garden. We know from the last words of the Passion read on Good Friday that the tomb of our Lord was in a garden (Jn 19:41). This is not an unimportant detail, because salvation history can be understood as a story of gardens.

We find three essential elements in a garden: order, beauty, and life. Order sets a garden apart from the wilderness. Its boundaries and design establish it as a specific place unlike any other. Second, a garden has beauty—a diversity of flowers and plants, colors, sizes, and shapes that pleases the eye. Finally, a garden has life. Plants grow and bear fruit, and animals find their territory a pleasing place to live.

This is what God desired for us in that first garden, the Garden of Eden: order, beauty, and life. Order, not just of the Garden, but of our own lives. He established us in a harmonious (well-ordered) relationship with Him, which bestowed in turn a harmony within ourselves and with others, the integration of soul and body, man and woman, man and creation. Likewise the beauty of that first Garden was not of the plants and flowers but of our souls, the surpassing beauty of the only creature created in His image and likeness. And He bestowed life there as well—the unending life with God.

By his sin Adam rejected the Gardener and lost the goods of the Garden. We have lost order, beauty, and life. Rebellion against God has thrown His creation into disarray. We now find soul pitted against body, man against woman, and all of creation at odds with man. It has brought the ugliness and horror of sin into the world. Most of all, it has brought death into the world, death in place of life.

In a second garden our Lord began the restoration, the redemption; Jesus went "where there was a garden, which he and his disciples entered" (Jn 18:1; cf. Mt 26:30; Mk 14:26; Lk 22:39). He entered the Garden of Gethsemane to undo the rebellion of the Garden of Eden. In that garden he took upon himself all the disorder, ugliness, and death that sin brought into the world. The entirety of it rushed upon and into Him. "And being in an agony he prayed more earnestly; and his sweat became like great drops of blood falling down upon the ground" (Lk 22:44). He Who is Beauty Itself became the Man of sorrows. He "who knew no sin" became sin for us (2 Cor 5:21). Life itself became death.

In a third garden our Lord continues His work—by rising from the dead. How fitting that His tomb should be in a garden—to complete the restoration of God's original plan. Indeed, when she first sees Him, Mary Magdalene takes our Lord to be the gardener (Jn 20:15). And in a certain sense, He is. He rises as the divine Gardener, to restore order, beauty, and life.

He completes His work in a fourth garden: the human soul. He desires to enter our souls by His grace and dwell within as the divine Gardener. He desires to reestablish within us His gifts of order, beauty, and life intended from the beginning—order, to heal that division and discord within us that produces all the division and discord outside of us; beauty, to rid us of the ugliness of sin and grant us the glory of His children; and life, that our hearts become lively and life-giving.

On Easter Day Mary Magdalene found Him in a garden. He rose in a garden so that we can in turn find Him within us, establishing His new garden of grace.

"Christians, Haste Your Vows to Pay"

The familiar hymn "Christ the Lord Is Risen Today" is a loose translation of the Easter Sequence (*Victimae paschali laudes*). The hymn exhorts us, "Christians, haste your vows to pay." Although the original Latin has nothing about "haste", the translator's poetic license hits the mark: Easter calls us to a certain swiftness and alacrity.

Indeed, everyone seems to be in a hurry in light of the Resurrection. On Easter Sunday Mary Magdalene runs back from the empty tomb to tell the Apostles. Then Peter and John run to see for themselves (Jn 20:1–10). The two disciples who encounter Jesus in Emmaus "rose that same hour" (Lk 24:33)—back to Jerusalem to tell the rest. Later, at the Sea of Tiberias, when Peter learns that it is our Lord standing on the shore, he immediately jumps out of the boat and into the sea and hurries to the shore (Jn 21:7).

Running can indicate different things: fear, competition, or urgency. The story of Philippides, one of the most famous runners in history, sheds light on its meaning. He was the legendary messenger who ran twenty-five miles from Marathon to Athens to announce the victory of the Greeks over the Persians. "Joy to you, we have won!"[7] he said—and then died on the spot. This example from antiquity hints at the meaning of the Easter races: the Apostles and disciples learn of Christ's victory, and they race to share their joy.

But in the end Philippides can give only a hint. The Christian reality outpaces the pagan image. The joy that inspires the running of the Apostles and disciples is about victory, not over any earthly power, but over death itself. It is a *spiritual alacrity* for the risen Lord—both to see Him and to make Him known. The Apostles and disciples hasten to see for themselves and then to bring the news to others.

Of course, this swiftness at Easter simply calls our attention to what should be a constant in the Christian life. In Saint Paul's words, we are to "run that you may obtain it" (1 Cor 9:24). Hebrews exhorts us to "lay aside every weight, and sin which clings so closely, and let us run with perseverance the race that is set before us" (Heb 12:1).

This Easter alacrity—meant to be a staple in our lives—serves as the proper remedy for our spiritual torpor. The creature comforts we enjoy (in a manner surpassing any other time in history) make us sluggish to prayer, lethargic in our devotions. We might respond to God's initiative—but not immediately, not with the swiftness that it deserves. And this languor is not neutral: if we do not run toward our

---

[7] Philippides quoted in John A. Lucas, *A History of the Marathon Race 490 B.C. to 1975*, at https://en.wikipedia.org/wiki/Pheidippides.

Lord, we will be overrun by sin. So it is that most of our culture's sins are really those of listlessness and sloth, of boredom with divine things, the refusal to stir ourselves to action for God. This spiritual somnolence becomes eventually a refusal of God's action within us. As the late Judge Robert Bork famously put it, we are "slouching towards Gomorrah".[8]

Ultimately, we hasten toward the things we love. And that should worry us terribly, because we race after all the wrong things: entertainment, physical pleasure, money, promotion, etc. And since those things are ultimately passing, we find ourselves not running toward something but just running in circles.

The ability to run the race, and persevere in it, is not our own doing. It comes from the grace merited on the Cross and bestowed at the Resurrection. As Saint Thomas observes, the gift of divine love "adds to natural love of God a certain quickness and joy".[9] The prophet Jeremiah gets a sense of the swiftness the Lord desires when he receives the rebuke, "If you have raced with men on foot, and they have wearied you, how will you compete with horses?" (Jer 12:5). Clearly, God intends this swiftness for more than just the natural order.

We hasten toward the things we love. Let us pray, then, that His Easter grace perfect love within us—to rouse us from our worldly stupor and make us run in the ways of perfection.

Going and Staying

"[B]ehold, I am with you always, to the close of the age" (Mt 28:20). It seems a strange thing for a man to say right before leaving. It is as if you said to your dinner hosts, "I must be going now and I will stay for dessert." Or a simple "Hello" as you walked out the door. This privilege to leave and to remain all at once belongs to God alone. He

---

[8] Robert Bork, *Slouching Towards Gomorrah: Modern Liberalism and American Decline* (New York: Regan Books, 1996).

[9] Thomas Aquinas, *Summa theologica* I–II, q. 109, art 3, ad 1.

does not remain with us as He did before. He really did leave us and ascend into heaven. And yet He promised to remain—a promise so strong that He speaks it in the present: "I am with you always, to the close of the age." So, how does He remain?

Sometimes we speak of people remaining with us even after they have left this world. "He lives in our memories," we might say. Or maybe we regard a person as still present by way of what he taught or accomplished. In some circles people have a more mystical view, thinking the deceased still somehow spiritually present. Now none of these captures exactly what our Lord meant by being with us always. In fact, they emphasize the difference of His presence from all others. He is with us not merely by memory or teaching or in some fuzzy mystical way. He is present, rather, by His Spirit and through the Church's teachings and sacraments.

As regards the Spirit, our Lord's parting words point to the essential connection between the Ascension and Pentecost, between His departure and sending of the Holy Spirit. He ascends in order to send the Holy Spirit. "I tell you the truth: it is to your advantage that I go away, for if I do not go away, the Counselor will not come to you; but if I go, I will send him to you" (Jn 16:7). It is by the gift of the Holy Spirit—His Spirit—that He remains with us.

This same Spirit makes Jesus present in and through His Church. At the Annunciation the Holy Spirit overshadowed the Virgin Mary, and she conceived Him within her womb. At Pentecost the Holy Spirit again descends, this time upon the disciples, to form Jesus' corporate Body, the Church. This helps us to deepen our understanding of the Church, which is not merely a gathering of His followers to remember Him and reminisce about old times. She is not just an organization for the mere continuation of His teachings. She is His Body, His continuing presence throughout the world and throughout history. Everything that He thought, said, and did in His human nature two thousand years ago He continues to do now by way of His ecclesial Body.

Notice that before ascending He charges His disciples with two tasks: to teach ("make disciples ... teaching them") and to sanctify ("baptizing them") (Mt 28:19–20). Or, put differently, the Church is to make Him present by way of her teaching and the sacraments. This is a unique mission.

In other regards we might continue the teachings of the deceased, and in that way maintain some kind of moral union with them. But the Holy Spirit gives to the Church alone the power not merely to convey Jesus' teachings but to teach in His name, with His authority, indeed as Christ Himself. The Church does not merely communicate Jesus' teaching. Christ Himself teaches through her.

Likewise with the sacraments. In other instances we may preserve the memory of the deceased by rituals, holidays, and other observances. The Church's memorial of her Founder, however, is not a mere reminiscence of Him. It is the actual making present of Him—of His life, death, and Resurrection. This is the reality of the sacraments, and most of all the Mass. They are not mere rituals or reminiscences, as we have in the secular world. They make Him and His grace present. By way of them the Spirit accomplishes in the Church what human memory can only attempt: the real presence of the One remembered.

"I am with you always," He says as He leaves. And by the gift of the Spirit He brings this promise to fulfillment, continuing His presence through the Church's teachings and sacraments.

APPENDIX 1

Funeral Homily for Justice Antonin Scalia[1]

We are gathered here because of one man. A man known personally to many of us, known only by reputation to even more; a man loved by many, scorned by others; a man known for great controversy, and for great compassion. That man, of course, is Jesus of Nazareth.

It is He Whom we proclaim: Jesus Christ, Son of the Father, born of the Virgin Mary, crucified, buried, risen, seated at the right hand of the Father. It is because of Him, because of *His* life, death, and Resurrection, that we do not mourn as those who have no hope, but in confidence we commend Antonin Scalia to the mercy of God.

Scripture says, "Jesus Christ is the same yesterday, today and forever" [Heb 13:8]. And that sets a good course for our thoughts and our prayers here today. In effect, we look in three directions: to yesterday, in thanksgiving; to today, in petition; and into eternity with hope.

We look to Jesus Christ yesterday—that is, to the past—in thanksgiving for the blessings God bestowed upon Dad. In the past week, many have recounted what Dad did for them, but here today, we recount what God did for Dad—how He blessed him. We give thanks, first of all, for the atoning death and life-giving Resurrection of Jesus Christ. Our Lord died and rose not only for all of us, but also for each of us. And at this time we look to that yesterday of His death and His Resurrection, and we give thanks that He died and rose for Dad. Further, we give thanks that Jesus brought him to new life in Baptism, nourished him with the Eucharist, and healed him in the confessional. We give thanks that Jesus bestowed upon him fifty-five years of marriage to the woman he loved—a woman who could match him at every step, and even hold him accountable.

---

[1] This homily was given by Rev. Paul D. Scalia at the Basilica of the National Shrine of the Immaculate Conception, Washington, D.C., on February 20, 2016.

181

God blessed Dad with a deep Catholic faith—the conviction that Christ's presence and power continue in the world today through His Body, the Church. He loved the clarity and coherence of the Church's teaching. He treasured the Church's ceremonies, especially the beauty of her ancient worship. He trusted the power of the sacraments as the means of salvation—as Christ working within him for his salvation.

Although, one Saturday evening he did scold me for having heard confessions that afternoon. And I hope that is some source of consolation (if there are any lawyers present) that the roman collar was not a shield against his criticism. The issue that evening was not that I'd been hearing confessions, but that he'd found himself in my confessional line. And he quickly departed it. As he put it later, "Like heck if I'm confessing to you!" The feeling was mutual.

God blessed Dad, as is well known, with a love for his country. He knew well what a close-run thing the founding of our nation was. And he saw in that founding, as did the founders themselves, a blessing. A blessing quickly lost when faith is banned from the public square, or when we refuse to bring it there. So he understood that there is no conflict between loving God and loving one's country, between one's faith and one's public service. Dad understood that the deeper he went in his Catholic faith, the better a citizen and a public servant he became. God blessed him with a desire to be the country's good servant, *because* he was God's first.

We Scalias, however, give thanks for a particular blessing God bestowed. God blessed Dad with a love for his family. We have been thrilled to read and hear the many words of praise and admiration for him, his intellect, his writings, his speeches, his influence, and so on. But more important to us—and to him—is that he was Dad. He was the father that God gave us for the great adventure of family life. Sure, he forgot our names at times or mixed them up; but there *are* nine of us. He loved us, and sought to show that love, and sought to share the blessing of the faith he treasured. And he gave us one another, to have each other for support. That's the greatest wealth that parents can bestow, and right now we're particularly grateful for it.

So we look to the past, to Jesus Christ yesterday. We call to mind all of these blessings, and we give our Lord the honor and glory for them, for they are His work.

We look to Jesus today, in petition—to the present moment here and now, as we mourn the one we love and admire, the one whose absence pains us. Today we pray for him. We pray for the repose of his soul. We thank God for his goodness to Dad, as is right and just. But we also know that, although Dad believed, he did so imperfectly, like the rest of us. He tried to love God and neighbor but, like the rest of us, did so imperfectly. He was a practicing Catholic—practicing in the sense that he hadn't perfected it yet. Or, rather, that Christ was not yet perfected in him. And only those in whom Christ is brought to perfection can enter heaven. We are here then, to lend our prayers to that perfecting, to that final work of God's grace, in freeing Dad from every encumbrance of sin.

But don't take my word for it. Dad himself—not surprisingly—had something to say on the matter. Writing years ago to a Presbyterian minister whose funeral service he admired, he summarized quite nicely the pitfalls of funerals (and why he didn't like eulogies). He wrote, "Even when the deceased was an admirable person—indeed *especially* when the deceased was an admirable person—praise for his virtues can cause us to forget that we are praying for and giving thanks for God's inexplicable mercy to a sinner." Now, he would not have exempted himself from that. We are here, then, as he would want, to pray for God's inexplicable mercy to a sinner—to *this* sinner, Antonin Scalia. Let us not show him a false love and allow our admiration to deprive him of our prayers. We continue to show affection for him and do good for him by praying for him: that all stain of sin be washed away, that all wounds be healed, that he be purified of all that is not Christ. That he rest in peace.

Finally, we look to Jesus, forever, into eternity. Or, better, we consider our own place in eternity, and whether it will be with the Lord. Even as we pray for Dad to enter swiftly into eternal glory, we should be mindful of ourselves. Every funeral reminds us of just how thin the veil is, between this world and the next, between time and eternity, between the opportunity for conversion and the moment of judgment. So we cannot depart here unchanged. It makes no sense to celebrate God's goodness and mercy to Dad if we are not attentive and responsive to those realities in our own lives. We must allow this encounter with eternity to change us, to turn us from sin and toward the Lord. The English Dominican Father Bede Jarrett put it beautifully when he prayed, "O strong Son of God ... while You prepare a place for us, prepare us also for that happy place, that we may be with You and with those we love for all eternity."

"Jesus Christ is the same, yesterday, today and forever." My dear friends, this is also the structure of the Mass—the greatest prayer we can offer for Dad, because it's not our prayer but the Lord's. The Mass looks to Jesus yesterday. It reaches into the past—to the Last Supper, to the Crucifixion, to the Resurrection—and it makes those mysteries and their power present here, on this altar. Jesus himself becomes present here today, under the form of bread and wine, so that we can unite all of our prayers of thanksgiving, sorrow, and petition with Christ Himself, as an offering to the Father. And all of this, with a view to eternity—stretching toward heaven—where we hope to enjoy that perfect union with God himself and to see Dad again, and with him to rejoice in the communion of saints.

APPENDIX 2

Fides et Ratio, 5

Rather than make use of the human capacity to know the truth, modern philosophy has preferred to accentuate the ways in which this capacity is limited and conditioned.

This has given rise to different forms of agnosticism and relativism which have led philosophical research to lose its way in the shifting sands of widespread scepticism. Recent times have seen the rise to prominence of various doctrines which tend to devalue even the truths which had been judged certain. A legitimate plurality of positions has yielded to an undifferentiated pluralism, based upon the assumption that all positions are equally valid, which is one of today's most widespread symptoms of the lack of confidence in truth. Even certain conceptions of life coming from the East betray this lack of confidence, denying truth its exclusive character and assuming that truth reveals itself equally in different doctrines, even if they contradict one another. On this understanding, everything is reduced to opinion; and there is a sense of being adrift. While, on the one hand, philosophical thinking has succeeded in coming closer to the reality of human life and its forms of expression, it has also tended to pursue issues—existential, hermeneutical or linguistic—which ignore the radical question of the truth about personal existence, about being and about God. Hence we see among the men and women of our time, and not just in some philosophers, attitudes of widespread distrust of the human being's great capacity for knowledge. With a false modesty, people rest content with partial and provisional truths, no longer seeking to ask radical questions about the meaning and ultimate foundation of human, personal and social existence. In short, the hope that philosophy might be able to provide definitive answers to these questions has dwindled.[1]

---

[1] John Paul II, *Fides et Ratio*, September 14, 1998, https://w2.vatican.va/content/john-paul -ii/en/encyclicals/documents/hf_jp-ii_enc_14091998_fides-et-ratio.html.

APPENDIX 3

Saint Thomas Aquinas on Saint Joseph

According to many saints and theologians, such as Origen, Jerome, and Bernard, Saint Joseph sought to divorce Mary not due to suspicion of her infidelity but out of a reverential fear of her holiness. According to this interpretation, Joseph draws back from the Virgin Mother because he sees himself as unworthy of her. Saint Thomas Aquinas explains this interpretation as follows:

> [Joseph] did not suspect adultery: for Joseph knew Mary's chastity; he read in Scripture that a virgin would conceive: "And there shall come forth a rod (virga) out of the root of Jesse, and a flower shall rise up out of his root," etc., (Isaias 7, 14 & 11, 1). He also knew that Mary had descended of the line of David. Hence, he more easily believed this to be fulfilled in her, than for her to have been ravished. And therefore, considering himself to be unworthy to dwell with one of so great holiness, he wanted to put her away privately, as Peter said: "Depart from me, O Lord, for I am a sinful man" (Luke 5, 8). Whence, he was not willing to take her, that is to lead her home to himself, and accept her as a spouse, thinking himself to be unworthy.[1]

[1] Thomas Aquinas, *Commentary on the Gospel of Saint Matthew*, trans. Paul M. Kimball (Camillus, N.Y.: Dolorosa Press, 2012), 44–45.

CONTRIBUTORS

Helen M. Alvaré is a professor of law at George Mason University School of Law, where she teaches family law, law and religion, and property law. She publishes on matters concerning marriage, parenting, nonmarital households, and the First Amendment religion clauses. She is faculty advisor to the law school's *Civil Rights Law Journal* and the Latino/a Law Student Association, a consultor for the Pontifical Council of the Laity (Vatican City), an advisor to the United States Conference of Catholic Bishops (Washington, D.C.), founder of WomenSpeakforThemselves.com, and an ABC news consultant.

Raymond Arroyo is a *New York Times* best-selling author and a producer. He is the news director and lead anchor of EWTN News, the news division of the Eternal Word Television Network, a Catholic broadcast network founded by Mother Angelica, a nun of the Poor Clare order. He is creator and host of the news magazine *The World Over Live*.

Mary Ellen Bork is a freelance writer and lecturer on issues affecting Catholic life and culture. She serves on the advisory board of the School of Philosophy at Catholic University of America and of Christendom College. She serves on the editorial board of the magazine *Voices*. Her articles appear in the *National Catholic Register*, the *Washington Times*, *Voices*, and *The New Criterion*. Mrs. Bork, wife of the late Judge Robert Bork, lives in McLean, Virginia.

Rev. Paul Check was ordained a priest of the Diocese of Bridgeport, Connecticut, in 1997. He served as an officer in the U.S. Marine Corps for nine years prior to entering the seminary. In 2008, he was selected to succeed Father John Harvey as the executive director of Courage International, at the request of Father Harvey and with the approval of Bishop Lori and Cardinal Dolan. He spends much of his time traveling and making presentations to clergy about the Church's teaching about homosexuality and her pastoral response.

Scott Hahn, Ph.D., is a professor at Franciscan University of Steubenville. He is an exceptionally popular speaker and teacher. He has delivered numerous talks nationally and internationally on a wide variety of topics related to Scripture and the Catholic faith. Dr. Hahn has been married to Kimberly Hahn since 1979. He and Kimberly have six children and fourteen grandchildren.

Lizz Lovett lived a storybook romance with her husband and four kids in Portland, Oregon. With the help of Father Paul Scalia, she converted from Buddhism to Catholicism in 2005 and lived out her life faithfully. She delighted in sharing an early morning coffee with her husband, as well as enjoyed fishing and the salty sea air.

Dan Mattson lives in the Midwest, where he has a career in the arts. He is featured in the Courage Apostolate's documentary *Desire of the Everlasting Hills* and is often invited to share his testimony to clergy, schools, and parishes. He blogs at LetterstoChristopher.wordpress. com. Other writings may be found at *Joyful Pilgrims*.

Gloria Purvis is a speaker, Catholic television host, and mother. She has dedicated much of her life to sharing Church teaching on life and sexuality in the public forum. As a public speaker, she's given talks at youth conferences and on television news shows. In 2012, she helped host the EWTN television show "Authentically Free at Last", which discussed societal issues like marriage, abortion, contraception, and forming a Catholic conscience.

H. James Towey is the second president of Ave Maria University. His career has included service as a college president, senior advisor to the president of the United States, key aide to a Congressional leader, member of the cabinet of Florida's governor, founder of a national nonprofit organization, and legal counsel to Saint Teresa of Calcutta.